PADMAN

A Dad's Guide to Buying... Those
and other tales

Mark Elswick

From the Reflections of America Series

Modern History Press

From the Reflections of America Series

Library of Congress Cataloging-in-Publication Data

Elswick, Mark, 1969-
Padman : a dad's guide to buying-- those and other tales / by
Mark Elswick.
   p. cm. -- (Reflections of America series)
   ISBN 978-1-61599-115-0 (pbk. : alk. paper) -- ISBN 978-1-
61599-116-7 (hbk. : alk. paper) -- ISBN 978-1-61599-902-6
(ebook)
   1. Single fathers--United States--Anecdotes. 2. Fatherhood--
United States--Anecdotes. 3. Brain damage--Patients--United
States--Anecdotes. I. Title.
   HQ759.915.E57 2011
   306.874'2208740973--dc23
                                              2011032571

Published by
Modern History Press, an imprint of
Loving Healing Press
5145 Pontiac Trail
Ann Arbor, MI 48105

www.ModernHistoryPress.com
info@ModernHistoryPress.com
Tollfree USA/CAN: 888-761-6268

Distributed by Ingram Book Group (USA/CAN), Bertram's
Books (UK)

Dedication

This book is dedicated to two groups of people:

First, to Traumatic Brain Injury caregivers who face an unimaginable amount of stress every day.

Second, to the numerous military personnel who put their lives in harm's way so every one of us at home can feel safe and do what we do.

I salute all of you!

Contents

Acknowledgments

Thanks to these amazingly talented people:

Cover work:
Cover Design Copyright © 2011
www.DigitalDonna.com

Author Photos:
Scott LaForest Photography
Davison, MI

Editor:
Tyler Tichelaar
Marquette, MI

Special Thanks to the following, though this page is far too small to list everyone individually:
First, and foremost, my parents, Ralph and Sandy Elswick, who saw I was taken care of throughout my rehabilitative climb. Mom, Dad: I love you both.

Next, my family and friends: For all of the undying love and prayers.

Then, McLaren Outpatient Therapy Program for pushing me back to me. Just a couple of specific people to mention are

George Marzonie (physical therapist) and Rise Alexander (speech therapist).

Also, there's my hometown of Burton, Michigan (Burtucky). More specifically, thanks to the community, schools, teachers, and coaches of Bendle Community Schools for helping to instill the perseverance and drive in me never to stop striving.

Near the bottom but NOT in importance, I want to thank my daughter, Gabrielle Elswick. You made this book possible. I love you so much.

Finally, thank you to the U.S. Military. America salutes you for allowing us to do what we do. THANK YOU!

Preface

The reason I have written this book is twofold. First, it is because becoming an author has been a dream of mine for some time. However, due to uncontrollable circumstances, it is obvious that I wasn't able to do it for a long, long time. Now, I feel I am really able to put 100 percent into this, with my 100 percent finally being good enough. Next, and more importantly, this book is about giving back to Traumatic Brain Injury research, patients, and treatment. Answers and treatment plans for this quiet crippler often remain a mystery. Considering the onslaught of TBI cases we are about to see with our returning troops, shouldn't we better understand this injury and be more prepared?

I hope in these pages to entertain you with humorous stories taken from my life, but also to sprinkle in some more serious stories about my traumatic brain incident and other survivor stories. I'll use the humor to keep it light in hopes that you will read both the funny and the serious stories, laugh a lot and also learn a little.

A broken bone can heal *over time*. A cut scabs over and heals *over time*. A brain injury, traumatic or otherwise, can become psychologically, biologically, physically, emotionally, and even violently *worse over time*. The ramifications of such injuries, which range from mild to severe, leave one wondering how a small damaged area of a human brain can completely render the entire body defenseless and helpless.

With TBI patients' caregivers in mind, I have completed this mostly-humorous short story collection because I have witnessed how time-consuming, frustrating, and heartbreaking it can be for a caregiver to watch the life of a loved one be completely slowed or taken away. Obviously, smiles are much-needed and welcome necessities in the daily lives of these people. Therefore, the goal of my first book, leading to 2012's TBI-focused book, is simple: Mostly with humor, I want to alleviate some of the daily stress these caregivers face, while also providing more ammunition for researchers.

So, read this book and feel good about yourself, knowing that you bought a book that entertains you while you contributed much-needed finances to a growing problem in America, brain injury. You're being part of the solution!

"The U.S. Constitution doesn't guarantee happiness, only the pursuit of it. You have to catch up with it yourself."

—Benjamin Franklin

Padman: A Dad's Guide to Buying...Those

From the moment the words woke me, I was sure the mission I faced would be my most difficult to date. At 8:51 a.m., I was unexpectedly stirred in my comfortable bed by words every man dreads to hear from his daughter, girlfriend, or spouse. As unplanned and unfortunate as it was, today was my day, the day I realized that all men, albeit unknowingly, have a bit of Padman inside them.

The morning started with sheer shock. My daughter's first words to me were followed by complete silence as I gave an eye-opening response. As if we were both acting on the big screen, 007's suspenseful movie music began pulsating between my ears. Immediately, I shot her a glare—constant, almost piercing, and never before witnessed by her eyes. My inability to move—due to a combination of blinding sun beaming through the window and my daughter's words—forced a hypnotic glare from me that must have frightened her. Her words, however, were far more ferocious.

Just as James Bond himself has done on numerous occasions, I darted into action following that silent, momentary pause. However, let it be known that even though I compared my situation with all of 007's dangerous missions, having seen every Bond flick, I can assure my readers that the larger-than-life ladies man never faced the life-altering experience I was about to encounter for the first time. It, my friends, was man's greatest fear—coming face-to-face with feminine hygiene (FH).

"Dad, please go to the store for me," were my daughter's exact words on that not-so-memorable morning. But it was her subsequent words that truly shocked me, froze me, and nearly pierced my heart.

"I need pads—BAD!"

As those startling words awoke me, a slow, sinister, penetrating freeze began at my ears and continued to flow through my body to the tips of my toes. I felt cemented to my bed by an eerie feeling. Like a demonic possession, it consumed me. As I lay silently in my suddenly not-so-comfortable bed, trying to exhale, I realized I had become completely statuesque. After what must have been a forty-five second mesmerized state, my eyes finally blinked. Then, as if I had been shot out of a cannon, I sprang into action.

There I was, a single dad, about to do what virtually every man would agree was "the unthinkable." But like a trooper, I jumped out of bed almost instantly—well, instantly once I was able to move—when I heard the urgency in my little girl's voice. Without even showering and with no idea how to go about the task before me, I hurriedly got dressed, brushed my teeth, grabbed my coat, donned a baseball cap, and put on my sunglasses, hoping thereby to hide my identity, and away I went—off to face this heinous challenge.

As with any unenviable event Fate decrees, people usually remember exactly where they were when an unexpected crisis arose. For example, my aunts, uncles, and parents can all recite exactly where they were when they heard President Kennedy was assassinated. Still others, including myself, can pinpoint their exact locations when the media broadcast that President Reagan had been shot. I would even go so far as to say that my fifth grade teacher, Mrs. Board, could recall how cloudy it was while Noah was busy building his boat. In fact, as a detailed example of cemented memory, I was an eight-year old playing at Granddad's when Channel 5 broke the news that The King had permanently left the building. I can remember the precise channel and television location in his small living room as I rushed into the house at the sound of my mother's scream on that dark, August day in 1977.

Now with a twelve-year-old daughter, today would prove to be yet another example of cemented memory. As much as I wish I could, I will never be able to forget my exact location, the scenery, and the spine-tingling feeling that I endured during my inaugural FH Day. The sun was shining brightly, but as is common in Michigan, the wind was extremely brisk. It looked like spring, but it felt like January in Alaska. Being covered from head-to-toe was the only thing shielding me from possible frostbite, windburn, and sunburn on this all-too-familiar morning of Michigan's eight-month-season we call winter. As brutal as it appeared to be, not even the elements could stand in my way as I *courageously*—I felt, anyhow—accepted and embarked upon this mission. Displaying nothing short of sheer determination to go along with a ruggedly resilient scowl, I sped to the nearest drugstore and waltzed right in, demanding what I needed. Looking back, though, I am not so sure that "demand" is absolutely the most appropriate term I could use. To be honest, whimper or murmur would be more accurate.

The mood quickly shifted from confident to flat out bleak once I was inside the all too "obscene" merchandise dealer. Trying to go unnoticed (even though I was the only shopper in the store), I tiptoed down every aisle, searching for the oldest working male I could find to help me locate the nasty quicker-picker-upper items, which shall remain nameless for the time being. Unquestionably, I was overcome with fear, not to mention a newfound insecurity I felt increase with every minute of my incognito navigation of the premises on quest for this "mythical" older, male pharmacist. I did not have a mirror, but I am quite positive that a growing look of despair was replacing my once-confident stare. Furthermore, I could feel my hard, stoic chin turning to quivering jelly as I slowly and quietly scanned each aisle. Out of nowhere, at that very instant of my helplessness, I felt the tiniest amount of Man Fluid build up in my eye and roll down my left nostril. In that woeful hour, I must have, somehow, sprung a leak. That was the precise moment when it occurred to me that "demand" had left my vocabulary. Right then and right there, I knew I would be forced to "beg" for assistance.

In sheer desperation, as I continued to scour the vicinity for this phar-*man*-acist, my sneaky suspicion was adding to my already bewildered state. I was mortified to discover there was, in reality, no older man working behind the counter. In fact, there was no male working in the store at all. Instead, four women were on the time clock. Working behind the counter were the manager (it said so on her name tag) and assistant manager (same thing). Then, working on the floor in aisles one and six were two extremely attractive sales clerks who appeared to be in their mid-twenties. Since the managers were obviously "too busy," engrossed in what appeared to be empty boxes behind the counter, remaining oblivious to my world of pain and embarrassment, you know who I was forced to question.

Then, an image of Mike Tyson sprang into my mind. At that very instant—like the ringing of the bell for the opening round—I stomped my feet with each step and prepared to battle the inevitable. After all, every—and I do mean *every*—Padman virgin has faced the same decision. If you are a man who has yet to experience his initial run-in with buying feminine hygiene products, the following three alternatives are what will cross your mind, just as they crossed mine:

A) Leave the store and hurry to another where a fellow superior-species member can help.

The true reality of alternative A follows:

This course of action would be cowardly, despite it being one to which many members of the "stronger gender" often succumb.

B) Return home, get my daughter, and make her go in to buy "them."

The harsh reality of alternative B follows:

As demoralizing as it might be, I knew this option was not a real alternative. Between my teeth brushing and coat grabbing, I had asked her to go with me. Her response had almost made me hurl:

"Daddddddddddd????? I can't go! The toilet paper I'm using is already leaking."

To this day, those words and the expression she gave me still make me shiver.

C) Seek help right then, right there, from whatever female is available to assist; buy the pads, and become a "heroic" dad (at least in my own eyes).

The unfortunate reality of alternative C follows:

Though it was the most difficult, it was the *right* thing to do.

Basically, we men can stand, answer the bell, and come out swinging, or remain seated on the stool and throw in the towel. Since I had no Pad Cave to hide in, I chose the former of the two. Like the strong-willed man I was—or had thought myself to be—I decided to man-up, stick out my chest, hold my head high, and in the deepest voice I could muster, "demand" what I needed from an Eva Longoria look-alike.

"Excuse me, ma'am, but I...ummmmmmmm...pads some need for my aaaah twelve-year-old so... DAUGHTER! See, she... ummmmm... just... (not-so intelligent pause)... started and (fake two coughs)...I was stuck with coming to them buy (huge, yet not-so-subtle sigh, not realizing how ignorant and babyish I must have sounded to 'Eva')."

Probably because she detected my naivety, ignorance, and obvious insecurity, she had a hearty laugh at my expense. (You know the ones people try to disguise as a smiling cough?) Or, it could have even possibly been how my beet-red face went hand-in-hand with my futile masculine voiceover attempt. Undoubtedly, at that moment, I must have sounded like an amazing movie star, playing a nervous and shy fifteen-year old who was buying a condom from a grumpy, elderly female pharmacist.

"No problem. It's okay," she giggled before assuring me that my frightening mission was "normal" and proceeding to guide me to the grotesquely un-masculine boxes of... those... those... unmentionables.

As we turned the corner at the end of the aisle, I heard *007*'s music playing again—only louder this time. For the first time since I had entered that God-awful place, to which I will never return—not even for milk—my straight and stiff lips were beginning to form an upside-down frown while my jelly-like chin was quickly returning to its manly state. My independent solo mission was almost complete; I could sense it in my bones. I was back.

Feeling the confidence returning, I finally unzipped my coat on this short aisle-to-aisle jaunt. A quick glance out the window reminded me of just how gorgeous Michigan's winter sunshine was when it reflected off the beautiful, pure white snow. Also, outside the window, I could see rather large icicles hanging, yet slowly melting away as water dripped innocently below the window and out of sight. The beautiful icy water was fading from my vision ever-so sweetly, just like my fears.

Without missing a beat, I casually flipped my cap backwards—
I could now hear a rather large lady belting out a tune—after
all, this mission was about to be, triumphantly...over!

Then, as quickly as I had begun smiling in color, again,
civilization as I knew it stopped! The Fat Lady's tune came to a
screeching halt; this crisis was far from over. In fact, at that
very instant the theme music from *A Nightmare on Elm
Street*—or was it *Halloween*?—began to blare. In either case, it
had replaced my cocky 007 song.

Just when I had thought this incredible ordeal was at its
end, "Eva" and I reached the end of the aisle and she pointed
to the back wall. If not for the shelving of an aisle
perpendicular to the... the... those, I would have been a goner.
My knees buckled, my stomach turned, and my heart skipped a
beat (or two). To mention that she pointed at a space on the
back wall is just wrong, as all women will attest. As if she were
Vanna White showcasing every word in the dictionary, "Eva"
pointed to the *entire* back wall—not just a single section—the
entire back wall.

How on earth was I supposed to select the "right kind"? A
million different brands must have been on those shelves—
maybe two million. For four seconds, my wide-open mouth
must have looked to "Eva" as if I were catching flies. I silently
gazed at the wall in wonder as I grasped onto the shelf to keep
from dropping to the floor.

As if I were in the movie, *The Amityville Horror*, every fiber
in my body was crying, "Get Out...Get Out...!!!" But, the
newfound Padman inside of me refused to listen, even though
the male spirit inside of me was running for the door in a dead
sprint. That newfound "Padman" thingy made me stay.

Numerous husbands and fathers throughout the world have
faced the exact same three alternatives I had forced upon
myself earlier on this journey. However, just like so many of
my predecessors, I opted to stay and "fight." Subsequently, by
staying, I could actually feel myself morphing into...(insert

triumphant victory music HERE)...Padman! Of course, the change was unavoidable. There was no turning back. I had, as other men unknowingly have or will, now become *Padman: Conqueror of THE Fear*.

As I stood in awe, looking at the ridiculously large sea of Red Storm aids and Feminine Hygiene Products, I was in dire need of some help. Since "Eva" had returned to her busywork, I did what any true-blooded man would do: I pulled out my newly-named Electronic Communicative Device (ECD a.k.a. cell phone) from my Padbelt. As I reached to smash the first digit, my initial thought was to contact my daughter. Suddenly, however, I remembered how my once-angelic daughter had so casually alerted me that since it was only her "second cycle" (those words still make me cringe) she did not know what kind I should buy because last time she had "just used Mom's pads." (Feel free to puke, now. I spewed a chunk or two in my throat when I heard that.)

So, trying my hardest to remain calm in such a potentially catastrophic situation, I ECD'd her mother, who, horrifically, was not available. Then, with no alternative left, I relayed a message to a female friend of mine, who, for privacy issues, I will simply refer to as Padgirl X2HG. With twenty-plus years of personal FH expertise under her belt, literally, she was one of many in the female fraternity well-adjusted to the Mood Pendulum swings we men cannot understand. It doesn't take a scientific study to reveal man's inability to comprehend these irregular and unannounced personality transformations. And now, my daughter was experiencing the transformation!

All of a sudden, as if I had needed to feel even more frantic and mortified, Padgirl's response rolled across my ECD. It read: "You should really talk to her mom. You don't want to get the wrong kind."

Wrong Kind?

Really?

Obviously, that tidbit threw my Padman senses for a loop. Much like a quick ZOINK appearing on the TV screen for two seconds, those two words could have easily floored me had it not been for my new Padman determination.

Nonetheless, as a dad, even just a guy, who had never had any experience with this sort of thing, I did not understand how there could be two different kinds, much-less enough to fill an ocean. In my mid-thirties, I still swore there was no difference between Coke and Pepsi, Miracle Whip and Mayonnaise, or Butter and Margarine. How could there be this many "kinds" of pads? Aren't they all engineered to stop the same, despicable thing? Was I supposed to sort through boxes, trying to locate the right "kind?" Did I shake them by my ear like a kid at Christmas? After all, I did not want to return home with the "wrong kind."

Evaaaaaaaaaaaaaaaaaaaaaaaaaaaaaaaaaaaa!

Just before I started shedding tears, my ECD interrupted me. Thankfully, it was my ex. (I nearly cried a joyous tear; not since before the breakup had I been so happy to talk to her.) After I switched ECD channels to allow verbal communication, she politely explained what "kind" to buy. So, after breathing a sigh of relief, I hung up and hastily began to peruse the "Pad Section" for the designated devices. As I confidently browsed, I was all too happy to end this gruesome, yet surprisingly educational, episode.

Then, lo-and-behold, my heart stopped—yet, again! Could this day have gotten any worse?

It was something more grotesque than Dr. Hannibal Lecter could have envisioned in one of his cannibalistic plots. When I first saw it, my stomach and throat collided, forcing a sort-of hiccup—the kind often disguised as a burp. A few small grains of yesterday's lunch and dinner ascended to the back of my throat. If not for Padman's newfound and quick-reacting intestinal reflexes, last night's meal would have spewed all over the floor and onto the not-so-glowing diagram that screamed just two, puke-inducing words: "With Wings."

When you meet someone for the first time, but you have often heard about the person, a light bulb goes off in your head, "Oh, that's her!" Likewise, when solving a difficult problem that has you really frustrated, a light bulb will brighten over your head when you arrive at the long sought after answer.

That is what "With Wings" meant to me. I had no clue what W-squared meant before seeing the diabolical diagram on that box. Sure, most guys—myself included—have heard the term, but they never gave it any thought. In man-speak, Mike Tyson must have given "Buster" Douglass as much thought in boxing's epic, 1990-title upset. According to my far-from-professional opinion, these particular "artists" should be locked away in a dark dungeon for a very long time. Men do not conjure up this image for a reason. Likewise, I knew there was a good reason why I had never connected the dots to figure out what it meant. After all, there are just some things we men should not know and definitely should not see.

Awkwardly, I stood there like a fourth grade student trying to master advanced calculus; I knew only the basics, but that had been enough until this moment. Never had I delved into exploring what "With Wings" meant; nor did I care. At age thirty-four—a fully-grown man—I simply was not ready. (Insert actual tears.)

Because of my ex's final words on my ECD, I knew which box I had to buy. "Make sure you get them (yep) WITH WINGS." I had not realized that would be a problem for me—until horrendous "artwork" brought me face-to-face with what that two-word phrase actually meant. The judge's gavel smashed the instant the light bulb appeared above my head. I had, unwillingly, been sentenced into putting a *face with the name.*

With all of my male pride on the floor, I thought I was done after locating the "right kind." The store was dead silent, save more music on my brain's iPod, unheard by anyone except me. This time it was the soundtrack to an old western flick, starring Clint Eastwood or John Wayne. So, with my new-found Padman sensibilities, I turned to make my escape, albeit with a scowl of The Duke. There I went, carrying the box to the counter like a six-year old carrying a friend's cootie-infested shoe. The box was being given the ol' index finger-and-thumb carry, my hand touching no more than necessary. Like General Schwarzkopf planning a sneak attack, I strategic-ally made sure my finger did not go anywhere near that demented depiction while my thumb rested shyly against the box's front.

As usually occurs with a new Padman, paranoia began to set in. (Began??? To be honest, paranoia was cemented in me before I had left my house.) The aisle seemed to get wider and wider with every stride as I headed toward the counter. Perhaps someone was watching me, I thought. Undoubtedly, I was glowing with embarrassment that was obvious to every-one. Apparently, "Eva" had seen it too, judging by her giggles and laughs. However, none of that mattered now that I was finished. I could not be too careful and had to move rather quickly, making sure nobody saw me carrying...The Box.

I was determined not to let anyone rain on my parade with my mission complete. With my self-esteem about to be on the upswing, yet still displaying a lethargic and newfound shyness, I paid "Eva" for the—well, those. After she bagged the items, I was gone. Without saying as much as thanks, thank you, or have a good day, I exited the premises to the Padmobile.

As a grown man, I had no excuse to be so childish. That fifteen-minute, life-altering experience taught me that I, a manly-man, do—in fact—have inner fatherly powers of which I had been unaware, powers that virtually all men possess. Something as outrageous as that journey would have made many mere men crumble. But, the courageous dad inside all of us men is able to expose our inner Padman, retrieve... those, and safely provide them for our loved ones.

Looking back, I like to compare my former weakness for the FH aisle to a certain colleague's weakness for kryptonite. Before that bitterly cold day, I, just an ordinary man, could not even talk to a member of the opposite sex about—dare I say it—*periods* without feeling a biological meltdown. Now, having made my safe getaway from the drugstore, not only did I walk out a new, more secure man, but I had evolved into a real-life Padman.

P.S.: **Rookie Padmen:** Though you will proceed, undoubtedly, with caution throughout the store, double-bagging is not an absolute necessity when you escape the premises.

"Don't hate; it's too big a burden to bear."
—Dr. Martin Luther King, Jr

9/9, Again: Please ENNNDDDDDD!!!

September 9, 2010, 6 a.m.

The day started like any other morning...except for today's date. Just as every other September 9 has started, the walls seemed to be screaming, "Stay innnnnnnn! Stayyyyy innnnn!" as I rolled out of bed. September 9, 2010, marked the eighteenth anniversary of my life-changing and near-fatal automobile accident; it also marked the beginning of my nineteenth year of living with a Traumatic Brain Injury after doctors initially had said I wouldn't make it a single day.

Nearly two decades earlier, life as I had known it ended as the result of a devastating car accident that left me hanging on for dear life, in a coma and on life support. It all sounds pretty horrific, but thankfully, I can only imagine what happened during every second of my ordeal; no matter how I have tried remembering... nothing; those memories have been removed.

I am probably pretty lucky not to recollect any of it. My girlfriend at the time, nearly six months pregnant, was the only one with me that dark, early morning, so she has told me exactly what happened.

How I came to be in the actual place where the car hit me was quite bizarre. We had been driving down the road at roughly 7 a.m. With daylight just beginning to break, a car pulled out in front of us from a side road. Unable to react quickly enough, we slammed into that car, but none of us were hurt. The driver stopped his vehicle in the left-hand turning lane about twenty feet from my car, which sat parked on the side of the road. Then he ran back home, across the street, to call the police.

Meanwhile, my girlfriend and I stood on the roadside, waiting. Realizing my car's four-way blinkers weren't on, I went back to start them. As I reached my car, an oncoming driver was distracted from paying attention to the road before him by the sight of the abandoned car in the turning lane. While gawking at the abandoned car, he rear-ended the driver's side of my car hard enough to total my four-door vehicle. I had just opened the driver's side door to reach in and turn on the blinking lights when the collision occurred.

I only remember hearing my girlfriend scream, "MARKKKKKKK!!!!" as his car slammed into me. She watched as the impact threw me face first onto the hood. My head slammed into the windshield, and then my body was thrown eight feet into the air by the collision's momentum, followed by gravity sending me crashing to the pavement, head first. After the vehicle played pinball with my head, I lay motionless in the street. In a pool of my own blood, my gruesome injuries were evident—except for the brain injury.

Unbelievably, since I have no memory of the accident, it was not the most painful part of my ordeal.

An hour later, I was in a coma, sleeping in what doctors predicted would be my final resting place. A respirator was forced down my throat, an intracranial pressure monitor (ICP) was screwed into my head following surgery on my fractured skull; a brace around my neck stabilized me, a rotating bed kept me from getting bed sores, and both of my eyes were swollen shut; the left side of my face showed visible signs of a surgically-repaired orbital ring, and my left leg had a steel rod inserted into it. A life-support machine kept me breathing. Obviously, I was in quite a bit of pain and shock, which is why I'm happy I don't remember any of it.

But neither were the bodily injuries the most painful part.

Immediately after my parents arrived at the hospital with my girlfriend, doctors called them into a private room. There, they were told to get my brothers and sisters to the hospital because I would "not make it through the day." Later on, following a week of life support, they were warned that I would be a vegetable "if" I ever did come out of the coma.

Looking back at being on a life-support machine for a week and being a lost cause, I can only imagine how my family and friends must have felt as they hopelessly hoped. I can honestly say I would be scared to watch a loved one lying helplessly in a hospital bed like that. I am sure it had to be the worst feeling imaginable, knowing there was nothing they could do to help. I have often wondered who had it worse, my family and friends or me. Sure, I had all the physical complications and what-not, but they had to witness it, watch it, worry about it, not knowing whether I was going to make it. Meanwhile, I was in la-la land, unaware of what was taking place.

Can you imagine being told that your child or someone you love will either die or be a "vegetable"? Sadly, traumatic brain injuries (TBI) occur more often than one would imagine. They are always right around the corner or in *your* house.

Looking back now, the entire morning of September 9, the hospital stay, and the subsequent years of outpatient therapy were not even the most painful parts.

I did live, obviously. And, I did not become a vegetable, but suddenly, in my early twenties, I was forced to learn how to live again. By live, I don't mean "party" and "live it up." I mean L-I-V-E, as in how to think rationally, speak audibly, concentrate, memorize, walk, and even eat. At times, these everyday chores felt like extreme challenges.

At 6'1", I weighed a consistent 190 pounds before the accident. I was always doing some sort of physical activity to stay *at* that weight. However, after a month of being fed through IVs without moving, I was weighed on a scale. Since I could not walk or stand, it was a special scale that weighed me in my wheelchair. Unsurprisingly, since I was simply a sitting stickman, just "skin and bones" from what I've been told, I had lost nearly 50 pounds. Obviously, I was in need of some "real" food.

My first memory after coming out of the coma is about food. Since I had "woken" up just two days prior, my dad and others were in my room, still celebrating. They had been eating donuts. Unable to speak clearly or audibly, I mumbled and motioned that I wanted one. Everyone, including myself, was pretty excited from what I was later told. After all, it was the first solid food I had eaten since before my accident. Well, Dad broke the nutty in half and brought it to me. Little did he or anyone else know that I would take it, bite, and...swallow.

Where was the chew?

That's right, there wasn't one. With me gagging and coughing, everyone in the room was patting my back and giving me Eating 101 tips. That instant started my climb back, re-learning how to do everything most people take for granted in life.

Yet another instance of regaining my independence came in the bathroom, of all places. One day, I had to urinate. No more bed pans for me, I thought, full of male pride, aka stubbornness. I was determined I was going to take care of this situation myself. My mom, the only one in the room with me at the time, offered to help, but refusing, I wheeled my chair into the bathroom and tried to stand up to pee. As a man, there was no way I was going to sit. I *had* to regain my independence. Needless to say, I stood, trying to balance on my "good" leg while aiming. But, since I had not stood on my leg in over a month, I crashed to the bathroom floor almost instantly. Startled, my mom came rushing in. Thankfully, it was nothing serious; I was fine. But my wounded pride made me realize I was going to need a lot of help to get the new me back to resembling the old me.

Believe it or not, not even forgetting to chew, being unable to pee "like a man," or having to relearn any of life's other little "taken-for-granteds" were not the most painful parts, either.

When I was finally released from the hospital, my road back to normalcy became even longer and more frustrating. Confined to a wheelchair, I was unable to stand for periods of time. At times, physical therapists made learning how to walk agonizing. For instance, they would make me stand next to a wall, hold a rail with my left hand, and *force* me to try to "rip" out ten squats.

Piece of cake, right?

Oh so wrong!

Dropping my butt to my heels and rising, repeatedly, is something I will never forget; it is probably the most painful thing I have ever endured. By the time I reached two, call me a wuss if you want, I was almost in tears. Multiply that number by five and the pain was almost unbearable. Just ten knee bends would have me sweating profusely and close to tears.

After the grueling squats were eventually mastered, I was "forced" to walk turtle-slow on a treadmill for one minute while holding onto each side of the machine. I've never felt the pain, burning, and fatigue that tri-athletes must feel over the final mile of a triathlon race, but I have no doubt that the sensation in my legs during those minutes allowed me to experience what they must go through.

Don't let anyone fool you; physical therapists can seem downright cold and heartless to their patients, but they are absolute Godsends. Magically, though, my physical therapists had me walking by myself in amazing time. Thanks to some incredible work with them, just over four months after my accident, I took my first unsupervised and unassisted steps. The day I stopped using a cane is a day I will never forget. My girlfriend had not yet gone into labor, so she was to be induced on January 11. The night of the 10th, I hung my cane in the closet, saying, "My baby will never see me unable to walk." I have never used that stick again.

Getting my leg strength back enough to put one unassisted foot in front of the other was torturous. However, that is still not the most painful part of my TBI.

Brain injured. Unable to walk. Unable to talk. Individuals with these and other afflictions can relate to the horrific treatment of disabled individuals in everyday society. I'll go so far as to say that it really makes me sick the way disabled people are treated. Quite frankly, it makes me as mad as....For example, with doctors' notes in hand stating I was unable to work, concentrate, stand for periods of time, etc., not to mention my speech sounding like Charlie Brown's teacher, I was denied Social Security benefits (SSI) three times before finally winning my case. Additionally, finding a handicapped parking spot was next-to impossible because so many healthy people would rather steal a handicapped spot than walk an extra fifteen feet. A police officer will pull someone over for not using a blinker to switch lanes (guilty) or going five-miles-per hour over the speed limit (guilty), but how many actually look to give tickets to people illegally parked in handicapped spots?

Perhaps most visible on this list is how the government and society treat disabled individuals. I do love my country, and I feel fortunate to live in the greatest country on earth. However, with all of the difficulties I faced walking, talking, and thinking, I had to struggle to get any amount of State help or aid. If not for family and friends, I would have been homeless, unemployable, and a lost cause. (And, yes, there are brain-injured victims who, unfortunately, fall into that crack.) Conversely, if I were a twenty-year-old woman who had four or five kids by four or five different guys, then I would be getting state money, food stamps, Wic, Bridge, or any number of other food assistance and financial help programs available. Or, if I were a Third World country, I would be plastered all over the newspapers and television screens while this great country sent relief. As a tax-paying American, why was I treated like I had lost my rights to any financial help simply because I became disabled?

The capacity of people to be rude, nasty, and not to care will always be my biggest beef resulting from my traumatic brain injury. But, it's definitely not last in my *Huh?* category. Nor is the mysterious and often humiliating treatment of disabled individuals the most painful part for me, even though it is a very close runner-up.

I ask you to remember, whenever you encounter a disabled individual, that the old adage really is true: *You cannot judge a book by its cover*. I have been told that I, technically, will be considered disabled forever. To look at me, though, most wouldn't guess anything was wrong because all my injuries are housed inside my skull. Even though I am paranoid about people, worry too much, am nervous a lot, am overly impulsive, walk with a slight limp, can barely even jog, talk with a speech impediment, get scared beyond belief with every headache I feel, have poor concentration skills, have less-than-adequate attention habits, have a horrible short-term memory, have a disturbing variation of balance, have an almost comical lack of hand-eye coordination, and live in constant fear that, out of the blue, the proverbial *other shoe* will finally fall in my brain, I consider myself, much like Lou Gehrig, "the luckiest man on the face of the earth."

Looking back over the past eighteen years, despite my aforementioned tale of woe, I now get to meet more TBI survivors and hear more and more of their stories; they reinforce how fortunate I am to have recovered as well as I have. Unfairly, many other patients who have been in my shoes will never make it as far. When people see and hear me, the most noticeable problem I have is a speech impediment. It's safe to say no one could guess I was ever an inch from death's door. Unfortunately, my injury's "invisibility" plus the lack of understanding from others is exactly why a brain injury is considered a quiet crippler or silent killer. Because outsiders cannot see the pain or deficiencies, unless someone suffers from a brain injury, it is impossible to comprehend the mental complications involved in doing everyday "normal" things.

September 9, 11 p.m.

It is now nearly September 10 on the calendar. I have another hour—sixty minutes, just 3,600 seconds—to go before this horrible day is over.

And, that, my friends, is by far the most painful part of the injury. It's the same thing every September 9, of every year. I wake up, shower, eat, go to work, come home, do daily chores, watch TV at night, then go to bed. But, just knowing that today is *that* day makes it a horrible day. In my mind, I can't help but think of all the what-ifs and might-have-beens. On this particular day every year, I am probably the most safety conscious person on the face of the earth. Every year, I constantly count down the time.

HURRRRRRRRRRYYYYYYYYYYY CLOCK!

"Confidence is contagious.
So is lack of confidence."
                    —Vince Lombardi

Not Quite a Cure

Infuriated and tired, I dialed his number. The phone seemed to be ringing so slowly. Angrily, I figured Bill was ignoring my call, via Caller I.D. Surprisingly, though, he finally did pick up the phone, and I immediately began screaming.

Even though I had known Bill my entire life, this was absolutely going to be the end of our "doctor-patient" relationship/friendship. He was anything but a doctor, so I don't know why I ever listened to him in the first place. What had transpired just thirty minutes earlier solidified the fact that I had no plans of ever speaking to him again after this phone call. What he had conned me into doing was not one bit funny to me.

There I stood, a sick, and except for my stained sweatshirt, butt-naked man, freezing and screaming into the phone. The consequence of the sinister scheme he had led me to believe would cure my ills was so disgustingly wrong that it was *unforgivable*.

Making matters worse was what he was currently doing on the other end of the line. In the most evil, I-knew-it fashion, he was laughing uncontrollably.

I had first called Bill nearly a half-hour ago. At that moment, all I could think of was how my sick state had me feeling like I was in my final hours. First, there had been the pulsating pounding in my head, often accompanied by a rising and lowering of my body's thermostat. Then, there was my irritable and nauseously queasy stomach that made food seem like the last thing on earth I would ever want. The worst, however, were the hot and cold sweats, which were controlled by my internal dysfunctioning temperature gauge.

The symptoms had me more temperamental than a woman in menopause. This time of year could have only meant one thing: Flu Season!

I had the flu, all right, Bill diagnosed. As I knew from my own previous experience, this "bug" oftentimes makes us men feel like we are going to do one of three things:

> A) Catch on fire
> B) Have our heads spontaneously combust
> C) Die

The only questions as far as I was concerned were, "Which?" and "When?"

"My head is killing me. I'm hot, then cold, then hot, then cold," I went on and on to Bill, pouring my medical symptoms into our initial telephone conversation. "My throat feels like I'm swallowing sandpaper every time I swallow, and my stomach feels like it's being stabbed with a fork. I feel like death."

Then, with Dr. Greg House-seriousness, my lifelong "best" friend began to unfold his devilish plot. In complete sincerity, he promised me that his advice would cure me. Needless to say, it backfired—just as he planned.

"Get some orange juice, like a half gallon, and drink it as fast as you can, without stopping. The faster the citrus acid fills your stomach, the more apt it is to ward off the virus."

Like most other men, Bill included, I was pretty naïve about medicine and healing remedies. Therefore, because I am such a guy, any advice I am given is *official*, in my eyes. And, luckily for me, I just happened to have some O.J. in my fridge.

After getting off the phone to go try this miracle cure my friend had so caringly prescribed, I raced to the kitchen and pulled out the unopened carton of orange juice from the refrigerator. What ensued is almost too comical and too disgusting for anyone to think it believable. However, before I share the consequences of this fast-acting "remedy," I want to emphasize that every word of this story is gospel.

Alone in the house, I figured I would do what all men do when nobody can catch them: Drink straight out of the carton. After all, it was *only* a half-gallon, so why dirty a glass, right? After taking the juice out of the refrigerator, with my left arm propping my weak and sickly body against the counter, I unscrewed the cap of the supposed human elixir. Then, I commenced chugging. As the citrus potion was leaving the carton, it was filling my body with nourishing power—or so I believed.

The orange juice was making me feel like a certain sailor in a classic cartoon. He was instantly revitalized when downing his remedy; likewise, "Well, blowsch me away!" I felt the juice doing the same for me.

Just when I was beginning to feel stronger, my knees buckled beneath me. I refused to give in, though. Like Philadelphia's son, Rocky Balboa, I refused to quit. I continued to chug the juice until the entire carton was almost empty. Through my half-closed and droopy eyelids, I could see the carton emptying. With the juice entering my body, I began having visions of playing Balboa in the scene where he downed raw eggs for breakfast. For me, orange juice sufficiently replaced eggs as I imagined "Eye of the Tiger" blaring in the background. Meanwhile, the revitalizing liquid continued to splash down each side of my mouth and all over my sweatshirt. With Survivor's famous song building momentum in my mind, I heard Bill's advice yet again.

"Get some orange juice, like a half-gallon, and drink it as fast as you can, without stopping. The faster the citrus acid fills your stomach, the more apt it is to ward off the virus."

Like a trooper, I had drunk until the last drop. I was feeling as proud as if I had just scaled Mt. Everest and stood atop the world, confidently looking over my conquest. Following those final gulps, I victoriously slammed the empty carton down on the counter like the champion I felt I was, then wiped my mouth with my sleeve. I smiled, confident that the healing elixir would kick in and have me feeling up to my old self in a jiffy.

Nonchalantly, I pitched the empty carton in the trash and headed back to lie down on the couch.

That was when the full consequence of his medical "advice" hit me. During my eight-step jaunt to the couch, something strange happened that I truly hope never, ever happens again.

"Hello," my stomach seemed to start out saying in a weird, distorted, and muffled voice. Quite surprisingly, though, it did not quite say, "Hello." It sounded more like a demon burping the first four letters of the word. As I entered the living room, the noise, comparable only to something groaned by Linda Blair in *The Exorcist*, stopped me in my tracks. Mind you, wearing raggedy sweatpants, an orange juice-stained sweatshirt, and having lain in bed for the last thirteen hours, I was feeling pretty rough.

This demonic voice in the pit of my stomach forced me to stop, immediately. I simply could not move, paralyzed by fear. Not knowing what to do, I stood there, looking at a spot on the wall. As if I were posing with the Heisman Trophy, I was cemented in that very familiar stance, my eyeballs the only things able to move without repercussions.

Whereas I had envisioned the orange juice starting at my toes and re-filling my entire body with zeal and enthusiasm, it did no such thing. In fact, it did the opposite.

As I stood there with one foot off the ground, my stomach burped the final demonic letter of that word it had recently started. This time it was different. Not only was the O.J. not traveling throughout my body, and subsequently, reenergizing me, but it had now traveled downward as far as it could possibly go. The half-gallon had seemingly gone past my stomach, and with only one place left to go, it wanted out. Obviously, now, one can tell which room this story is heading toward.

There I stood in the entryway to the living room—just me striking a pose. But with the relocation of the juice demanding to come out my anal cavity *"NOW!"* I had to balance myself on one leg, a knee in the air, my butt cheeks clenched together tighter than Shaquille O'Neal in a Volkswagen. I looked down the hall to my right—the bathroom was just a few steps away. I simply stood there, frozen, wondering when it would be safe to move.

Have you ever had that feeling right in your gut, well, just a little south of there, actually, and been too scared to move from fear of unleashing the feces flood gates? Well, that was the exact reason I still stood there with one foot in the air. I couldn't put it down or it would have been like a push button on the floor. That's right; the gates would have swung wide open.

Like a statue supplying target practice for pigeon droppings, I was forced to wait it out. It felt as if I stood there a full forty-five minutes. In actuality, it was probably more like thirty seconds.

Then, out of nowhere, with the courage of David when he stoned Goliath, I stepped toward the floor. When the tiniest amount of pressure subsided in my stomach, I was confidently able to complete my stride. Much to my relief, there was no push button.

Then, with no time to waste, I quickly began the March of the Penguins to the bathroom. Normally, it would have taken me five, six, maybe seven steps. However, employing my newfound Arctic waddle, it took me at least seventeen heel-to-toe paces. (I think...counting them was the last thing on my mind.)

Once in the bathroom, I backed myself up to the front of the Royal Throne, ready just to bend my knees and squat on the commode. Thinking myself a man of decent intelligence, I am pretty embarrassed to admit how much time I had to spend thinking this part through. Before I could start maneuvering my *life-saving* plan, that feeling of not being able to move a muscle reared its ugly head once more. I was not about to waste a second as I calculated each phase of my strategy during Freeze-Mode.

Since I was simply wearing sweatpants, I concluded I could easily pull them off in less than a second. I figured I would un-tie the string of my sweats, drop my drawers, and squat on the Throne at the exact moment the gates holding back the enemy were released.

As I prepared to put into action my un-Einsteinian plot, I grabbed the string to untie my drawers and yank them down. One must not forget that I had precisely calculated the untying to occur just one millisecond before I bent my knees, signaling the breaking of the dam that was holding *everything,* and I do mean *everything,* inside. That way, The Browns would finally reach the Super Bowl on my posterior's way down to the seat. Once I set the plan into motion, there would be no backing out; it was do-or-die. The entire plan had less than one second to be executed.

Unfortunately, it seems that the string keeping my sweatpants tied had a mind of its own. I did not even consider what could possibly happen next if....

So, with my caboose backed up to the porcelain god as this perfect plan went into motion, I exhaled as much as I could. Then, as if the Green Flag were lowered at Indy, I pulled the string, squatted, began to drop my drawers, and the game plan went exactly as scheduled—except for one major detail.

I had not thought that when I pulled the string, it *might* be in a knot. And as I activated my well-planned scheme, it *was* in a knot; my drawers did not come untied. Subsequently, as I squatted, my sweat pants only came down about halfway on my backside. And, since the unglamorous flood gates were forcibly released, (I told you there was no turning back once the operation commenced) the U.S. Marines themselves could not have held back the disgusting intruders.

That's right. Without going into too many grotesque details, I will just say that the Browns failed to make the Super Bowl, yet again. That team went to the outer edges of the Bowl, all over the floor, and even covered the official Super Bowl apparel. Unfortunately, they did not make The Big Bowl.

In hindsight, that is one mistake I will never make again. Yes, I will always make sure the string is never in a knot, of course. But I will never again take such advice.

As bad as the horrible remedy Bill prescribed me was, there is still quite a lesson to be learned from this story. That is, simply, if a good friend is sick, you can suggest a doctor, cold medicine, steam vapors for the nose, or anything else. As readers notice, this is something that only guys would do to each other. So, men, if you really want to be a "friend," give some tried-and-true medicinal advice:

"Get some orange juice, like a half-gallon, and drink it as fast as you can, without stopping. The faster the citrus acid fills your stomach, the more apt it is to ward off the virus."

Then, just sit back and wait for that inevitable return call.

Oh yes, quite angrily, it *will* be returned.

"My doctor gave me six months to live, but when I couldn't pay the bill, he gave me six more months."

—Walter Matheau

Cancer Patients Need Your... Support!

March 30, 2010

8 p.m.

For one day, I had planned to give stats, be by-the-book, and write a no-nonsense story about cancer. Then, I would ideally stuff it down any reader's throat. Hard-nosed facts and sad stories would surely bring readers to their knees in fear. After all, isn't that the only way people, especially men, take notice of potentially dangerous things? Hence my favorite saying about people: "People are like wheelbarrows. They don't move unless pushed."

One such attention-garnering horror story that would push people to act was told to me by a nurse at the Genesee Hematology Oncology Institute (GHOI). She, literally, forced a five-second pause in our conversation. She told me the story of a twenty-six-year-old man who lived in Northern Michigan. For most twenty-somethings, cancer is not a concern. Agreed? Anyhow, he had found a "lump" on his testicle. Embarrassed, he was afraid to have it checked by a doctor. A little over a year later, embarrassment became the last thing on his mind. Once he FINALLY did have it checked out, he had waited too long. He became a statistic of testicular cancer discovered too late. Could his premature death have been avoided if he had only gone to the doctor, immediately, before it was too late?

Obviously, I had found a great lead to my story.

But WAITTTTTTTTTTTTTTTT!!!
Wrong!

If it were about sharing the numerous available morbid statistics, gruesome stories, and agonizing numbers, this story would be sad, but ordinary. Instead, a heartwarming story about how some brave breast cancer patients avoided becoming statistics seemed more appropriate after my visit to the GHOI.

- As just one of the previously cited "avoiders," a friend of mine, Laura Deville Sherman, "L.D." as she is affectionately called, courageously faced her final day of grueling chemotherapy. The smiles and laughter were much-needed in the face of this deadly disease.

- Similarly, Cris Gibson sat where L.D. had recently been. With ten out of sixteen treatments out of the way after that day, Cris was well on her way to becoming a cancer conqueror.

- Then, there was Debbie Landskroener who was sitting in a chemo seat for her first of six treatments. Like Cris, she was well on her way, too.

None of the aforementioned trio will ever become a statistic because:

- First, they were checked *early* after inspection.

- Next, they saw a doctor, immediately.

- Then, each has all of the willpower necessary to defeat this ugly monster.

- Finally, and arguably most important, each has a strong and reliable support system.

It may, in fact, surprise many to learn just how much emotional support actually means to cancer sufferers. So, read this story and take note of how much these people laughed in the face of one of life's biggest scares. Then, you decide how much you care.

If you know anyone battling this monster, I can confidently say that person needs your support. Take time out of your busy, but healthy, lifestyle to visit, talk, or just comfort him or her. Seeing the faces of these patients made one thing obvious: Laughter truly is the best medicine.

March 30, 2010

9 a.m.

Picked up L.D. at her house. After a couple of other morning stops, she and I were going to her final chemotherapy session.

9:30 a.m.

Went to my place of employment to visit several co-workers and students. The visit was amazing for L.D. and really seemed to lift her spirits. Interacting with several people seemed to be the perfect recipe to cheer her up as she prepared herself to face the agonizing after-effects of chemotherapy.

10:30 a.m.

Went to eat breakfast at a restaurant. We had set a time of 10:30 to meet another friend, T., there.

11:15 a.m.

Went to Farmer's Market to buy a small cake for another chemo patient, Cris, because it was her birthday. Unfortunately, we settled for a bouquet since there were no cakes.

11:35 a.m.

With T. following us there, L.D. and I arrived at the Genesee Hematology Oncology Institute. Knowing it was the last day she would have to visit there as a patient had her extremely giddy.

11:40 a.m.

The chemo day officially began.

With L.D. in her La-Z-Boy recliner on wheels—that was how all patients were administered chemo treatments through IV-looking bags—T. and I pulled up a chair and we all just began talking. We discussed school, life, kids, news, friends, the weather, and oh yeah, of course, Facebook. (They're addicts!) Meanwhile, T. was snapping a "mandatory" picture every so often. All told, she took eighty photos in three-and-a-half hours.

11:50 a.m.

Not long after sinking into her comfy chair, I began to think we were going to lose L.D.

NOOOOOOOOOOO!!!

WAITTTTTTTT!!!

Not that type of "lose." The Benadryl being pumped into her before the actual toxic stuff was making her woozy and tired. I thought she was going to fall asleep, for sure. Even though she started to nod off—she sure became "loopy" over the next ten minutes—the excitement of almost being "done" kept her going.

Noon

At this time, I really began thinking about this story's direction. Talking with patients and nurses, it sickened me to learn how insensitive some people are about this potentially fatal disease. It did not surprise me because I've witnessed how cold-hearted some people can be, but nonetheless, it was just wrong.

"A lot of men feel that breast cancer is contagious," Nurse Pam Long added about a supposedly-common myth among men. "I don't know why, but they hear that C-word and they don't know how to deal with it. They don't deal with illnesses, period!"

Another oncology nurse elaborated on Long's assessment. She noted how some men really seem to pull away from the disease when that is the time, more than any other, that a breast cancer victim needs support. Fortunately for Debbie Landskroener, her husband, Bob is not one of those people.

"I think your willpower has a lot to do with it (recovery)," Debbie noted, "but just knowing that everybody is behind you and supports you just makes you feel better. It keeps you more positive about yourself and makes you want to beat it. Then, you know you can beat it."

Bob concurred.

"I think it's very important, for me if nothing else," he said, passionately speaking about supporting his wife through this challenging time. "I think she appreciates it and knows I'll do whatever needs to be done."

The more I talked to other people, the more obvious it became to me that only one thing could possibly rival medication, with all its pain and the lingering side effects of chemo. Contrary to popular opinion, it is, surprisingly, not medicine, shots, more chemo, or anything medically related at all, that can lead to healing. In fact, it is something each and every one of us is capable of giving. It is, quite simply... support.

Without any intentions of writing about support, I discovered that "support" had become the day's overlying theme. The continuous laughter in that room was infectious as it spread from the patients, to friends, to nurses, and doctors.

"It's huge, huge, huge," Mary Spinney RN, OCN, pointed out. "You do notice a lot of difference in patients' outcomes if they do not have a good moral-support system. Having people around helps the patients get through their treatments. You do notice a difference in how they tolerate it, too."

12:50 p.m.

Cris arrived for her 1:00 appointment. Having started with sixteen "chemo dates" scheduled, Cris was now down to five following today's visit. Needless to say, as her Facebook page indicates, she is "kicking cancer's ****." With the side-by-side support of her loving husband, Scott, Cris is confidently embracing each battle on the road to recovery.

"The first two were rough," she noted about the grueling chemo treatments, "but the last few haven't given me much trouble."

Over the next 140 minutes, L.D., Cris, and Debbie laughed so much one would think they were being given laughing gas. I could not help but see how the laughter in the patients' eyes and their ear-to-ear smiles exhibited that no treatment was greater than what they were given that day. They were letting loose, forgetting their condition, and not giving the equipment they were hooked up to a second thought; it was amazing.

A day that began without a direction for this writer ended with a huge lesson. The degree of support and love that cancer patients need throughout their uphill climb was never more evident than at G.H.O.I. from 1:00-3:20 that day.

Maybe it was the story told of Ragoo the Gerbel, the anal-entry bandit.

Maybe it was the laughing stuffed monkey on the floor.

Maybe it was the two celebration cakes.

Maybe it was seeing Scott wheeling the cart with two birthday cakes around the room like a popcorn vendor at the circus.

(He was chiming, "Fifty cents...piece of cake...fifty cents...piece of cake..." Then an hour later, he carried on the same routine, but inflation must have struck the room as he wheeled the cart around singing, "One dollar...piece of cake...one dollar...piece of cake...."

By the way, the next piece he sells will be his first. Even if he had made money, I think he was sending the profits overseas to save Ragoo.)

Maybe it was the victory lap that L.D. and I made by wheeling through the lobby, some rooms, and the main chemo room, even accidently into bathrooms. (Undoubtedly, staff has found some tire tracks on the floor by now. And, they know where they came from.)

Whatever it was, a smile was on everyone's face, all afternoon.

Support!

It is not about money; nor is it about gifts. Cancer patients need that emotional support that loved ones banded together were displaying that day. As long as they have support, they can find a solution to a problem. As Debbie Landskroener stated, "It just makes you feel better about yourself, knowing you're not alone."

L.D. and Cris echoed their new friends-for-life's sentiments by emphasizing how scary it is to think cancer could be a solo battle.

"Support is *everything*," L.D. started. "Knowing you're not alone and that your people love you makes the fight more bearable. Being alone is just scary, and it helps tremendously to know that I'm not alone."

"I have been blessed with an abundance of support from family, friends, and of course, my crazy husband," Cris pointed out with a smile. "I have been so amazed at the love I have received. It is so incredibly important to have that. Sometimes I feel like I can't take it anymore, and that is when my family and friends will pick me up and carry me through."

March 31, 2010

Looking back, I was fortunate enough to witness the entire rehabilitative spectrum in a single day. L.D. wrapped up her chemo trips to fight off the killer in festive fashion. Cris was on the downhill portion of her treatments. Landskroener was at the beginning of a sure-to-be-successful journey.

In the end, after wanting to write something serious and hardcore to make people understand the pain of cancer and chemo, I changed my mind. I figured I would just write about what happened on March 30, and leave it up to the readers to decide whether they care or not; I'm betting that most absolutely do.

If you have a loved one or a friend with cancer, PLEASE do not let that person fight this battle alone. Cancer is a scary word, not a death sentence. It is completely beatable with detection, medical help, willpower, and loving support.

That day proved, after all, to be quite an epic day for many of my friends—old and new—and for me. Eating a great breakfast, my first time in Farmer's Market, the numerous "photo ops" (Did I really just write that I had a photo op? I blame Scott and his friend, Ragoo, for that slip), wheeling L.D. on a hilarious and never-before-seen Victory Lap through the building, or watching her sign The Bench on the way out the door as so many cancer conquerors before her had done after their treatments ended, all made the day good...no—great...no—incredible...no—memorable...no—magical....

Well, really I'm at a loss because there is no one particular word. A combination of the previous words, ggredibicalble, might work best. But then aga....

WAIT!!! I got it!

Tomorrow!!!

That's the word I am going to use to sum up that amazing day. It was a fabulous tomorrow-kind-of day. Witnessing L.D.'s ordeal made me realize the C-word is not a death sentence. In fact, with today's medicine, willpower, and loving support—which is nearly as important as medical help after diagnosis—there will always be a Tomorrow for every person diagnosed—if diagnosed early enough.

If worried...SEE A DOCTOR!

Do not wait and do it tomorrow!

Do it *FOR* tomorrow!

WIFE: "Before we got married, you told me you were well-off."

HUSBAND: "I was, and I didn't know it."

—Jacob Braude

Red Flags of Age

Well, it is finally official. I can finally admit that my daughter has been correct. I have, as she likes to point out, turned into an old man.

At 10:28 a.m., it became apparent to me. Yes, I have, indeed, morphed. If only I had seen the transformation occurring, I would have run far, far away to drink out of the Fountain of Youth. (Where is that, again?)

Reluctantly, I am finally admitting and waving the white flag for all to see. There is no sense in dodging the issue, anymore. It looks like my eighteen-year-old (going on forty in her mind) daughter was right on the money while I paid little attention to the red-flagged warning signs that should have been so obvious to me. I am now admitting that I am a forty-two-year-old fuddy-duddy—for lack of a better, more appropriate term. Throw my life's "cool" accolades out the window. I, my friends, am barreling down the highway to Old Man-ville.

I went from elementary Patrol Leader with Goober as my assistant and fifth-grade spelling bee champion (my classroom only; we had no ESPN appearance with India's winning geniuses back in The Day), to captain of the football team and prom king (I still wonder how that vote was tabulated in the pre-computer [heck, pre-electronic-device] days, to college graduate, to, well, my present state here in…GULP…Old Man-ville.

Like all other Old Man alerts, the first sign was obvious to everyone, except me. Before blowing the lid off the first red flag, let me ask, who does not like to be comfortable and cool while mowing the yard? I like to mow my lawn in shorts and a t-shirt. Also, I like to wear my U of M (that would definitely be Michigan) flip-flops. But as virtually every grass-mowing hater knows, you do not wear *just* flip-flops or sandals while operating a lawn mower—it's dangerous. Some debris could fly at your feet, possibly mutilating them. But more importantly, it's virtually impossible to get tough grass and dirt stains scrubbed off of one's feet when wearing flip-flops. However, the glaring red flag arises with the rest of my attire. So, not caring what I look like (red flag #1), I always mow my yard in shorts, t-shirt, hat, sunglasses, flip-flops, and...(insert sigh)...black socks. (#1)

Just knowing that I am dressing this way to prevent dirt and grass stains on my feet, instead of just wearing old tennis shoes and socks, should allow me to wave that O.M. (Old Man) flag proudly. Blindly, however, I never realized my attire *was such a blatant* red flag.

As if that were not enough, another sign that I am becoming a relic occurred a couple of nights ago. (I do not know how to keep this G-rated, but I will do my best.) I had been working and sweating in the blazing sun all day long. On top of a tar-filled roof with some friends and family members, we were putting all new shingles on top of my cousin's house. Since I worked behind a desk in a university, this type of manual labor was beyond exhausting. I had eaten only one meal that day and felt as if I had lost ten pounds. That night, I came home exhausted. My girlfriend stopped over to see me after I returned. To make a long story short, let's just say that she wanted to ride the roller coaster at my amusement park. Unfortunately, the coaster refused to pull out of the depot. No more "yankee my wankee, the Donger need"...sleep. I was beyond exhausted. More than a red alert, there! That little blue pill would not have even stirred me; I went right to sleep—olddddddd. (#2)

The final nail (flag) in my Old Man-ville trilogy tomb was hammered this morning at 10:28. It became apparent that I was no longer en route to that unavoidable place; that train had already pulled into the depot and I was just a passenger. I realized I had arrived while noticing how pathetically excited I became over—my new hole-punch.

Usually, my students ask to use my paper hole-puncher, and it is a big P.o.S. So, they use it, and like most college students, they complain and whine about it. But today, my boss delivered a new hole-punch. By no means is it the hole-punch I grew up with. (WOW! Who would have thought I would ever say that sentence in my lifetime? "It wasn't the hole-punch *that I grew up with.*"—another red flag.) This amazing new hole-punch is electronic; just plug it in, put up to fifteen sheets of paper into the tray, press a button, and voila! Remove perfectly punched paper, ready to be put into a three-ring notebook. Kids and students today have it so easy.

(Wait! Did I just write that last sentence, as well? WOW) (#3 and that last sentence could, easily, be viewed as #4.)

Would you listen to me? Sounding just like my dad's dad. I'm scared. I mean, I am not telling kids how "I walked four miles to school, every day, up a hill, both ways," or anything (yet), but…I'm just sayin'.

I am going to stop there because I am feeling like, well—I already admitted it earlier. So, it should not be a problem, right? Just give me a little time to become comfortable with my newfound status in life, which I am begrudgingly embarking upon. After all, eight-tracks were not replaced by CD's overnight. Gasoline did not rise from $0.58/gallon to $4.00/gallon in one day, either. Nor, am I going to be comfortable being a full-fledged o… ol… you know, overnight. I should, in the next few days—maybe weeks—nah, months, become more content and secure about this new state in which

I am living. Do not be surprised that it may take a while for my full-fledged acceptance. Remember, I am—after all—a proud, card-carrying member of the Procrastinator's Anonymous Club. So who knows when I will be able freely and openly to live up to this o... ol...you know.

Until that time, look for that guy mowing his lawn in Bermuda shorts, a T-shirt, flip-flops, and black athletic socks pulled up to his knees; it will probably be me. Right now, I am going outside to sit on the porch swing and drink some cold ice tea.

"You can observe a lot by watching."
                                    —Yogi Berra

Frogger Shopping

Ever feel like you are the main character in a video game? Ever feel like you're doing things, only to realize that, in all actuality, a Higher Being must be controlling your every move?

At this year's annual morning-after-Thanksgiving debacle, commonly known as Black Friday, I was that game pawn. While I believed I was making moves of my own choosing, I now have no doubt I was being maneuvered to safety by some supernatural force.

Anyone knowing anything about video games created in the '80s knows exactly the game in which I was the pawn. We all played it back then as kids, but today, as adults, we are being played. Yes, my friends, I was the frog. The beginning, middle, and end of this year's post-Turkey Day shopping event was tedious, time-consuming, and unpleasant.

When we first arrived at the mall parking lot, I could have cried. My girlfriend, in the passenger seat—you know, the one where the people with the most navigating wisdom (in their minds) sit—was being a not-so-perfect co-pilot. Quite sarcastically, it was almost awe-inspiring how she used her female know-it-all powers to verbalize the movement of every car in the parking lot. She had told me before, but until now I'd never seen evidence of it—she really did have ESP. If you don't believe me, ask her. Ask any other female, and she will tell you the same.

It was amazing how at 4 a.m. she could know everything that everyone was going to do. For instance, I cannot begin to count the number of times we were slowly creeping up a crowded lane, hoping to find a parking spot. Then, out of nowhere—like a voice from Above—came her verbal warnings. "He's backing out," "Watch it; she's turning," or my personal favorite, "Slow down! You're going to miss something."

HUH?????

Did I have on a blindfold?

She firmly believed that these not-so melodic orations were accident saving. Wisely, I did not have the heart to point out just how whiney-sounding and annoying her navigational instructions were. Typically, a voice that I "love" to hear, her pleas were not so welcome on this I'd-rather-be-in-bed shopping excursion.

I guess I should be thankful. After all, if not for her, how else would I have ever noticed *potential disasters*? In fact, if there had been no all-knowing female in my car, I might still be looking for a spot—or so she would have everyone believe.

After finally finding a parking spot, in the back of the lot, we entered the mall. That was when I realized no greater time exists to appreciate manners than the festive shopping season. Each and every one of us was taught manners and etiquette, but most forget these admirable traits at this time of year. In fact, the most welcomed expression I heard that day was the rare, "Excuse me!" I heard plenty of other expressions, but I cannot, in good conscience, write them here. Suffice to say, I was cut off, bumped out of the way, told to move, and ordered to wait. And, those were just the friendly comments…from my girlfriend.

I wouldn't say that the day was all bad. The holiday season is a bonding time for sisters, husbands and wives, parents and children, and friends and neighbors, right?

Wrong!

As much as it pains me to say it, if given the choice, I would rush to a hospital and sign a waiver for immediate amputation of my left hand rather than ever again go shopping on the morning after Thanksgiving. Waiting for the mall doors to open, I stood in line outside for three excruciating hours in bone-chilling cold weather when I could have been home catching some much-needed sleep.

Most would think it must have been worth it since we would have gotten a lot of shopping accomplished after The Wait. Not the case! In all, we visited—count 'em—three stores.

Purchases?

We made three. We bought a remote-control car for my nephew, a CD for myself, and an LCD TV for my girlfriend's mom. Quite a day of holiday bliss, eh?

Finally, we were leaving. After being called every name in the book, and seeing some rude, mean, and barely-legal behavior, we were done. I will never, as long as I live, understand why people can become so despicable while they are shopping. I don't think I can ever forget those mothers and grandmothers…it was awful, just awful.

As an example—one I am not too proud of—I was reaching to grab my dad a running suit. Unfortunately, I did not reach fast enough—or should I say strongly enough. In the midst of shoulder-to-shoulder shoppers, the suit was literally yanked out of my hand. Astonished, I looked at my girlfriend, who was being pushed against me by the mob.

"It's okay," she assured me. "Let it go, honey."

Honey????

Wow! From the way she had said that word, maybe this day would turn out all right after all. I had gone shopping with her like she wanted and now we were heading back home. Looked like reward time for the big guy; I was all smiles.

And as she asked, I let it go…for a minute.

As we were making our getaway from the crime scene, with a silly grin on my face and her clinging to my right arm, we bumped into the running suit thief. After getting a good look at the person, I was certain the incident was not this particular shopper's first run-in with a moral issue.

But, I had promised to let it go, and I was determined to do so without causing a scene.

"You tried taking my suit, you schmuck," the blunt wrongdoer shouted at me for everyone to hear.

"Ma'am," I calmly replied, (Yes, it was a woman, but she was awful big and burly—way bigger than me.) "You got the suit, so let's just move on."

But she was obviously more experienced than I at these sorts of things—namely, shopping and brawling. In a raspy voice so deep that it made Barry White sound like a high-pitched tweeting bird, she blurted out:

"Stay outta my way, if you know what's good for ya, sonny!"

Was this the roller derby?

So what if she were in her seventies? She had an extremely intimidating aura. Throughout our entire interaction, she was intimating that she would whack me upside the head with her purse if I got in her way again...and it was one big pocketbook.

Quickly, not to mention angrily (All right! Make no mistake; I was scared.), I turned to leave. Like a little schoolgirl, I pleaded with my girlfriend.

"I'm done, baby. Can we please go, *now*?"

Thankfully, after patting me on the back, she agreed to leave.

Wait...patted?

Was I three?

My life and limbs had just been threatened. Did she not realize the severity of this? I had every right to be a little shaken—especially after the psychotic old bat had hoisted a deadly weapon to tease me. And I could tell she was not afraid to use it.

Before we could make our final getaway, we had to wait in a line that was like a maze of dominos lined up around every corner and down aisles. We spent more time in line than we did actually shopping. In two of the stores, we had to wait in those mind-spinning lines; the other store was just a bumping center for us. If I guessed, I'd have to say that we spent over an hour in the checkout lines of both stores, painfully inching our way toward the cash registers.

After starting, stopping, dodging right and left, and backing up, we were finally making our getaway. Somehow we got through the line at the checkout, and then, we were out the door and staring at the parking lot. It had seemed like there were a ton of cars when we had arrived. Now, there must have been a ton-and-a-half. Many of the vehicles were hopelessly trying to find a parking spot in the overcrowded steel jungle. I did not care. It was 9:00 a.m. and I was leaving.

Holding hands, we walked out of the building and onto the sidewalk. If we had not been holding hands, I would have lost my girlfriend. Talking to me, she nearly stepped in front of an oncoming vehicle. Some maniac was flying down the first row. I yanked her out of harm's way as this "moron," driving the unheard of speed of 15 mph, paid neither us nor other customers any attention.

We went forward three steps before backtracking one as a car slowly passed. We waited for it to pass before sliding left four paces and waiting on another to pass. After that, we jumped forward three more steps. However, traffic was now coming from the opposite direction. We were forced to back up a little and let one car drive by. We stepped up, and finally, were facing our final obstacle. I will admit it—a bit of adrenaline rushed through my body. After a little jostling right and left, we raced across the lane and reached the parking lot. Safe at last!

At that point I realized we had just been playing a game of human Frogger. All holiday shoppers play this—especially in the wild mall parking lots as shoppers try to find a place to park and mall store checkout lines as other shoppers maneuver around the congested retailers. But rather than dodge logs, insects, and alligators, we had been dodging shopping carts with the power to make a grown man cry when blasted against his shin and jumping out of the way of live vehicles that could crush and maim.

"The man who does not read good books has no advantage over the man who can't read them."

—Mark Twain

The Four-Letter Word Men Hate Hearing...From Women

Over the weekend I learned that I am, by male birthright, an important sounding board for women. After reading this story, I am sure most guys will agree, and I hope women will be better able to understand what we guys are thinking while in "listening mode." Though we love you and love to communicate, just as women poke fun at men for certain things, this is one topic where women deserve to be poked. Be the female a friend, girlfriend, fiancée, wife, or whatever, women sure can talk. Maybe it is simply that there is, in fact, such a thing as the *Gift of the Gab*. However, that's one gift I could go without ever opening.

On a night out with my girlfriend, I found myself forced to participate in a ninety-minute "listening session," a chunk of my day I'll never get back. As should be done with all trying times in life, I attempted to make the best of it. Honestly, though, I ended up learning something very important for us guys. I discovered one simple word to be as vile as all of the other four-letter words people shouldn't use. And you can add this word to the top of a man's list of things we hope never to hear, especially from a woman's mouth.

It all began at 7:48 p.m. I remember the time because I looked at the clock right when she started telling her not-so-earth-shattering tale. Little did I know that by asking one simple question, I would receive a one-and-a-half hour response. Sure, I gave the occasional head nod, smile, frown, "no way," and "uh-huh," just like we men do to pretend we're following along. However, she was completely oblivious to the fact that while she prattled on, I was planning out my schedule for the entire upcoming week in my head, while rewinding last week's events, mulling over the career path I had chosen, thinking about breakfast that morning and dinner the next night, wondering why my parents had named me Mark, laughing at some of the funnier commercials I'd recently seen, contemplating the problems that my Detroit Tigers were having...and fixing them! and going through the 2011 season schedule, wondering whether my Lions would manage to win a few games this year. Heck, I even heard two brand new songs on the radio.

The evening had started innocently and ordinarily enough. We had grabbed some fast food and were on our way to have a drink or two at a local establishment. On the way there, I asked her a simple question. (Yeah right!) If she would have only said yes or no, we could have moved on and continued an extremely enjoyable evening.

But, noooooooo! This was a woman, after all.

What ensued told me to brace myself and hold on tight, for the ride was about to begin. Everything started to move in slow motion. You know how things go ultra-slow in the movies and the characters "Taaalllllllkkkkkkkk lllllllliiiiiiiiiiikkkkkkkkkkeeeeee tttttthhhhhhhhiiiiiiiissssssssss????" Yeah, it was that kind of weird slo-mo.

As we pulled into the parking lot at 7:48, I asked whether she had gotten a chance to watch a movie the night before that she had been wanting to see. It was a simple, straightforward question, right?

Wrong!

As if I were a director, she answered the yes/no question as if I had just commanded, "Andddddddd ACT!"

She took her hand off of her soda in the console and everything began moving in super, almost painful, slow motion. She reeeeaaaacccccheeeeddd ffffooooorrrrrr tttthhhhheeeee radio knob to turn it down. It was still audible, but she didn't want it turned up, creating a chance that she would not be understood completely. Then, in addition to the slow-mo, it was as if the spotlight were turned on to illuminate her in the darkness. She looked at me with a sweet smile and began.

"Wwwweeeellllllllll," she started....

Ninety minutes later, I had my answer: Yes! She did see the movie, and she liked it. In fact, the made-for-TV movie was apparently so memorable that she remembered every single line from the flick.

So, women specifically, riddle me this!

Why did a question that could have been answered with a yes or no response turn into a ninety-minute soliloquy? I'm not saying I don't want to talk or communicate, but c'mon. Like most other guys, we'll talk and listen, but there is a limit.

So, with that particular "listening" session over, I ran inside and finally escaped the horror that virtually all men call a living Hades. Women simply call these sessions "communication."

In case readers haven't figured out what the one word is that wreaked such havoc on my evening, here it is: That single four-letter word that men hate to hear coming from a woman's lips is simply..."Then." I think I heard "Then," at least thirty-four times in the car that night; I actually lost count at seven; the conversation became a blur after that. Every time I thought she was done talking and we were going into the club–BAM–she would do it again. She would perk up with that radiant smile and booming from her lips, in super slo-mo, would come another, "Thhhhhheeeeeeeennnnnnn."

In the end, after all was said and done, it turned out to be a pretty good night. Unfortunately though, immediately after dinner was, well, brutal. Then....

Gotcha!

There is no more. After all, I am a guy.

"Happiness is not a goal, it's a byproduct."
—Eleanor Roosevelt

Newborn to Dad: NO Multi-Tasking!

Ever wonder how the phrase, "He looked like he'd seen a ghost," came into existence? Well, the first night my newborn daughter, Elle, was home from the hospital provided this new dad with a rude awakening. It was at that point I realized that doing things within my own timeframe were now in my rearview mirror. Although I was trying to keep one eye on her and the other on the TV, she quickly gained my undivided attention. As I screamed for help, I looked exactly like I had, well, seen a ghost.

As a new father, imagine encountering something from your newborn that is utterly shocking, something never-before seen. How scared would you be? How would you react?

Calm?

Cool?

I don't think so! At least not if you were a guy in my socks on this occasion. After all, I was just a young dad with no experience at this sort of thing. What my baby girl did was to initiate me into the many comical situations parenting would bring.

That one particular night, Elle did something that, quite frankly, scared the...well, you know the rest...out of me. Assuredly, as my girlfriend can attest, I could not have been whiter had I actually seen my grandma sit up in her grave.

On my baby's first night home, she wasted little time in educating her dad. Without even trying, she began teaching me that my multi-tasking days were over, especially with another female in the house. Reluctantly, like so many other young, naïve, strong-willed, and scared dads throughout the world, therein began my painful adjustment into what is known as fatherhood.

"I have to go to the bathroom," my girlfriend, Carrie, casually said as we were watching both TV and Elle. My daughter, oblivious to her newfound surroundings, was completely content in her mother's arms, until Carrie added, "Change her, please; she stinks."

This normally would not have created caution, but I was genuinely concerned. The love of my life had just returned from delivering a seven-pound bundle of joy. Getting up off of the couch where I was engaging in what I thought was some quite stimulating conversation with her, (Okay, fine. I was watching the basketball game and wouldn't have noticed if she had left the state) she assured me she was fine and just needed to use the restroom. Relieved, I expressed some genuine man concern in my response.

"Okay!"

Of course I would change Elle while Carrie was gone for a few minutes. I had to, didn't I? Just three days earlier, my baby had given birth to, well, my baby. Therefore, as a father, it was my duty to change her.

Then, as if the city dump were magically dumped next to me, Carrie handed Elle to me. Meanwhile, I caught the downwind smell of my daughter's gift package that nearly brought tears to my eyes. I now understood why Carrie, like many new mothers, had refused to let me change Elle during the first couple of days. Suddenly, though, she had all the faith in the world in me.

While Carrie made her exit, the game fortunately went to a commercial break. Not wanting to miss a minute of my program, I dived into my task with Mom-like quickness. (I know, I know, dive is probably the worst possible word choice.) This whole changing-a-poopy-diaper thing had me less than excited, even though it would be the first time I had changed her on my own. But I was happy that Carrie had finally found confidence in me.

She deserved any break she demanded, right? After all, through the entire labor, Carrie had been a real trooper. Even though she went through what looked and sounded like the most painful thing EVER—even more painful than falling off your bike seat as a twelve-year-old boy and racking your...on the "sissy bar" (#*!$#@^#!), I was so proud of how she had handled it all. And we were both extremely excited about raising our little girl.

Honestly, though, if it were me, there is no way I would ever have been able to endure what she did; I'm a guy— HELLO! Not only did I not have the right equipment for delivery, but—and much more importantly—I had, and have, that wimpish fear of pain that we members of the "dominant gender" are born with. To be honest, I don't think males could deal with childbirth. Despite how macho we claim to be, I don't know one of us who could endure labor pains. After all, I have seen smaller watermelons than babies. And, even those delicious summer fruits are not forced through a seashell-size hole.

So, after I mumbled my heartfelt word to Carrie, she skated toward the bathroom. I was, as any guy can understand, fully engrossed in Michigan State battling I.U. on T.V.; the winner would sit alone in first place. Being a huge basketball fan, this game was extremely important to me. One could have even classified it as that day's game of the decade. (Carrie just didn't understand about the next day's game of the decade or the next day or the next....) In fact, my dream had always been to have an All-American son playing for an iconic coach like Bobby Knight or Rick Pitino, so when Carrie and I had found out that she would not be giving birth to my superstar jock, my disappointment was, unfortunately, evident.

Not long after I was released from my own hospitalization due to an automobile accident, Carrie and I went to the ultra sound. Surprisingly, I left even more heartbroken than my physical injuries had caused me to be.

Like a buffoon—remember, it's a male gene we men are born with, so we have no control over some of our actions—I displayed my unhappiness with what-should-have-been-incredible news. Do not get me wrong; eighteen years later, there is no way I would trade Elle for a boy, not even my wished for all-American. But, at that time, I had just been involved in a life-threatening automobile accident and was experiencing the woe-is-me syndrome.

"Yep, she's definitely a girl," the over-joyous nurse reported with a smile.

Carrie, fighting her enthusiasm, shot me the most loving of looks. Her eyes twinkled as she smiled from ear to ear. I believe a halo even appeared above her head. This, truly, should have been a picture for a greeting card.

Needless to say, my response did not match hers.

"Figures," was all I said. With my luck lately—I had just been through a traumatic car accident—"Figures" seemed like the most appropriate thing to say at the time; I wanted a boy so badly. In my self-pity phase, I was not happy about the news of...a girl.

Note to all future fathers: Little girls rock. If you're lucky enough to be having a healthy girl, consider yourself fortunate.

So, on that first night home with Elle, as Carrie walked to the bathroom, I did not want to neglect my three-day-old angel. However, I did not want to miss this game, either. Like any *responsible dad,* I placed my right hand on my daughter's belly without turning my eyes from the TV. Because she was so tiny, my right hand covered more than her belly; it rested atop more than half of her body. My eyes, on the other hand, were glued to the television, to the left end of the sofa. In typical Dad Defense, she was secured.

"Honey, I have to take Elle in for a checkup tomorrow," Carrie's voice shouted from behind the open bathroom door.

My girlfriend, who had just gone through excruciating pain, was telling me something about the biggest addition to my world. Something so precious and sweet had already become the greatest thing in my life. In that all-too-familiar dad-like response, I let the love of my life know just how interested I was. They were just two words, but I know they revealed my true enthusiasm over life's other important matters—like the game that was on.

"Uh-huh," I bellowed back, hoping to shut her up until the next commercial.

Unbelievable, huh?

This woman had just given me the greatest gift I could ever receive. Everyone, including me, was so excited by Elle's arrival. I had a healthy three-day old daughter, but in man-like-fashion, all I could think of was a game. After all, the commercial had now ended.

Unbelievable is absolutely correct.

Then, without any sort of notice, things suddenly became very intense.

"Are you even watching her?" Carrie pleaded from the other room.

How was I to know that was not a rhetorical question? I'm just a guy. She was simply checking up, I figured. Elle was fine.

"She's going to roll off the couch," my mom-sounding girlfriend continued without waiting for an answer to the previous question.

Thankfully, though, there was a time out at that moment. And, as luck would have it, I was able to turn my head and give my *undivided* attention to the *ripe-diaper* task at hand.

"No, no, no baby," I assured Carrie with an unseen smile. "I have a good hold on her, and I'm barely even watching the game. I can hear it; that's enough for me."

I babbled to my infant in baby talk, laughing as I unstrapped the adhesive on each side of her diaper.

Suddenly, faster than I pulled the front of the diaper down, I slammed it back shut. Inside was a *mess* like I had never seen. Since Elle was the first child for both of us, the color, substance, and smell was all surprising, not to mention just wrong. How could a baby create such a *mess*?

I looked down to the floor at the wipes, hearing the game's return. Knowing I had to be Mom-quick to return my eyes, my left hand grabbed four wipes because this situation was, well, just gross. In fact, if I had rubber gloves, I would have worn them. Needless to say, I pulled the diaper back, quietly groaning and making a face the entire time, wiped a lot, bundled it all up for the garbage—outside garbage—and put a clean diaper under her, leaving it open. With her clean and secure and the dirty diaper on the floor, I returned my eyes to the game as I yelled what all men would yell after changing a gift package.

"Babe, can you come here? I got something I meant to give you earlier."

In an instant, Carrie returned and stood next to the couch, shaking her head and smiling as she realized what the *gift* was. As I leaned over to kiss my little girl's forehead, Carrie stood next to the sofa in another greeting card moment.

Unfortunately, at that exact time some really bad, almost evil, thoughts erased the perfect family picture. Even though the visions were years away, I was growing angrier by the second. Years later, I am still positive that all dads have this sort of experience. I did not like it one bit. Before my lips left my daughter's forehead, I was having the following deplorable Dad Visions:

What will I do when another boy kisses her?

What about when she goes on her first date?

Oh my God—what about her period? (That was my first Padman thought.)

Worst of all, how do I talk to her about things like...sex?

At that time, thankfully, I heard the announcer yell as someone drained a three-point shot with thirty-six seconds remaining. In typical guy-fashion, I became a cheerleader on the couch, a one-handed cheerleader.

"I'm going to take a bath," said the mother of my little princess, picking up the disgusting package and starting to walk away again. "Please keep a good eye on her. Turn off that stupid game!"

With that, she leaned over, kissed me gently, and sauntered into the bathroom. In turn, I kissed her back without even closing my eyes or taking my left eye off the TV. Our soft lips had met and the momentary lip-lock between new mother and father made it feel like time had stood still, or so one would think. Unsurprisingly, though, I felt a sense of relief as I immediately turned my attention back to the television when she exited the room.

Unfortunately, while in the bathroom, Carrie felt the need to long-distance converse. Why hadn't she just taken the phone with her? I had hoped she would just sit in the tub and have a much-deserved soak. Besides, the game still had less than one minute to go, which could be nineteen minutes in normal clock time.

"I'm hungry," she casually yelled, after she made her way into the bathtub. "Do you feel like ordering some pizza?"

"Uh-huh," I instinctively barked back.

"What do you want on it? Want anything else with it? I'm starving!" she blurted in one breath.

When I didn't respond for two seconds, her one-way conversation continued, interrupting my game even more.

"I think I want some breadsticks and a salad, too. Nah, make that antipasto salad."

State 57—I.U. 54...twenty-three seconds left.

Didn't she understand? This game was for the conference lead, first place! Please just be quiet for a few more minutes, I silently pleaded.

Then, like fingernails across a chalkboard, it came again.

"Honey, what do you want?"

"Uhhh-oonnnttt-ooo," I replied.

(Yeah, that really is a word in Man Dialogue. Its female equivalent is "I don't know," but it's faster in Man Dialogue.)

Honestly, I really didn't care. I should have just said that. I would have eaten anything...as long as it shut her up so I could watch the rest of the game. I never bugged or badgered her while she watched her talk shows and sitcoms. Why was she "bothering" me?

"Will you call and go get it, honey?" she asked.

State 58, I.U. 57....eleven seconds remaining (timeout).

Go get it? Did she forget about delivery? All I could think of was this game...and Elle, of course. Carrie knew how much I wanted to see this game, and then with eleven seconds left, she wanted me to leave? Furiously, I wanted to scream at her that there was no way I was leaving. SHE would have to order it and have it delivered.

"What?" I shouted, giving myself time to come up with a better plan to avoid the pizza run so I could keep watching T.V.

Then I heard the sound of running water, and the sound of her foot hitting the water. Before I could feel relief, however, I heard her turn off the faucet and step back out of the bathtub. My frantic nerves vibrated inside my body—the game was not over, and she was going to return, wanting to *talk*.

Noooooooooooooooo!!! It was too soon for her to leave the bath.

Sadly, I figured she had probably only bathed long enough to wash her hair.

With Elle sleeping comfortably under my palm, which incidentally, was the last time I had ever had my daughter in the palm of my hand, the game returned in the middle of Carrie's unclear and irrelevant mumbling. Ignoring her, my body increased two testosterone levels with the game's return from another commercial break for its final seconds.

Then, with my heart pounding, hands shaking, and wanting to scream and cheer, it happened.

With Carrie in another room, fresh from her hot and relaxing, albeit quick, bath, I felt, heard, and saw something more disturbing than I had ever witnessed in my life. Thinking she was oblivious to the goings on, Elle lay on her open diaper and demanded my attention at the exact time *my* game was coming to a climactic conclusion. At that moment, a ghost parading across my living room would not have disturbed my nerves as much as what Elle did to me. At age twenty-three, I just knew life still held a few more surprises for me. But, this was definitely one unwelcome surprise—not to mention, quite a scare.

"CARRIE...CARRIE...HELPPP!!!"

Still not dressed, my girlfriend came running into the living room, scared out of her ever-living mind. With her breasts jiggling every step of the way and wearing nothing but a frightened frown, she sprinted to Elle's side, looking like she was in the opening of a *Baywatch* episode. Her radiant energy allowed her to witness the grotesque disturbance for herself. Almost in tears—me, not her—my womanly-like screams were enough to summon a fire department. And this was no cat-in-the-tree emergency—this was real.

As Carrie's bouncing sexuality entered the living room, she found me frozen. It was as if poisonous venom were causing the wet spot on my thigh to expand from a dot to more and more and more....Okay, fine! So, it wasn't quite poisonous. But, it was taking over my right leg.

Amidst the chaos in our small living room, I was helpless to stop it; it was just one continuous—for lack of a better word—jet stream. The wet spot on my sweat pants was growing by the second. Unable to move, I turned to watch Elle just lay there with her baby smile, oblivious to the fact that she was peeing all over my leg.

Remember how I had told Carrie I would change Elle's diaper? Well, like all faithful, dedicated fathers, I was in the process of getting it done, right? Then, the game returned from a timeout. With no choice, (I'm a guy, remember!) I had stopped for a minute, failing to fasten the adhesive strips because I *had* to see the game. My hands were to my right, but my eyes were glued to the left (TV). That is what we men like to call multi-tasking.

It was obvious my little girl would never be one to suffer from *stage fright*. Obviously, she did not care, either. At just three days old, she was already *letting it fly*.

"Oh my God, Carrie," I continued to cry, loudly, as she laughingly covered Elle's urine stream with the towel that had been on her head.

"I didn't think girls could pee a jet stream out like that!" I whined.

Apparently, Carrie found it amusing—I might even say that she thought it was comical. She went from near tears, to near wetting herself from laughing so uncontrollably hard.

To me, there was nothing funny about it; I was scared. I felt the need to get in the shower. Looking like I had "seen a ghost," I now cared about the game as much as Elle did.

All-in-all, there is a valuable moral to this story. And obviously, it's an easy one to figure out.

"No matter how much of a multi-tasker a new dad may claim to be, newborn babies will find a way to show that those days are over!

"Never to suffer would be never to have been blessed."

—Edgar Allen Poe

In Front of Me?

"Dad, can we stop and pick up Jeff?" my thirteen-year-old daughter asked as we walked out the door to go to my nephew's elementary basketball game.

"Jeff?" I whispered as I froze, midway through locking the door.

Looking back, it's all sort of funny. Barely a teenage girl, Elle knew how I would respond to her having a male "friend" in our company. There were plenty of girls at her school for her to hang out with; I just did not understand why she needed a boy friend—ok fine, "boyfriend" (one word). And she knew I felt that way, which is why she waited until the last possible second, as we were leaving the house, to ask whether he could go with us.

"He's the boy I was telling you about. He goes to Kennedy High School."

EEEERRRRRRRRRRRRRRRR (Hold the presses!!!

Those last two words really caught my attention. Did she say "High School?" Without making a sound, I slowly withdrew the housekey, stood upright, and slowly turned my head to glare at her.

"Did you really say 'High School'?" I asked in my best Clint Eastwood voice. Meanwhile, the stoic look on my red face confirmed that she had been correct to wait until the last possible second to say anything.

"He's a sophomore," she ever-so-casually laughed. "He's only two years older than me. Besides, you're three years older than Mom."

With a playful slap on my arm, she headed to the passenger seat. I, on the other hand, just stood there. Had I said anything about her mom and me? This was about her! *Don't you go changing the subject!*

"High School?" I mumbled two more times.

"C'mon, Dad; we have to get Jeff."

Oh, yippee! I sarcastically rolled my eyes as I headed toward the car. I just *knew* this would not be a good idea.

"Do you want to stop and get some donuts?" I asked in a monotone voice as we backed out of the driveway. I was trying (man, it was hard!) to be a "cool" Dad.

"No! We don't have time. We have to get...."

"JEFF!" I loudly interrupted. "I get it. I get it. Tenth grade, though? Where's this MAN live?"

I don't know whether my sarcastic tone lightened the mood or she was just trying to shut me up, but she laughed quite a bit at that—Wait! Now that I think of it, she was a thirteen-year old—of course she was just trying to shut her dad up.

"It's on the corner of Oak and Brishphill. Make a right there and it's the first house on the left," she directed me.

I didn't do it, but I came so close to slamming on my brake right in the middle of the road. HOW DID SHE KNOW....

"Elle, honey," I said, calmly and lovingly attempting to switch emotion gears as I rounded the corner. "How, pray tell, do you know where this bo— man lives?"

In ultra-quick teen-girl fashion, she eased my rapidly growing aggression.

"He told me on the phone last night! DUH!"

SSSSHHHHHHHHEEEEEEEEEEEWWWWWWWWWW WW!!!

She was obviously clueless why I had asked the question as I wiped the sweat off my forehead and pulled into Jeff's driveway.

"DON'T YOU DARE HONK!" she screamed like a commanding officer ordering his soldiers to "HOLD YOUR FIRE!" As she climbed out of the car, she said, "I'll go to the door. But, Dad, when he gets in here...."

TRIVIA TIME: How many parental readers know exactly what her parting words to the dear driver will be? If I had to bet, I would say that well over 90 percent of all parents hear this phrase far too often. Before reading on, take a guess at what her next words will be.

...

...

"...you better *NOT* embarrass me!"

With that demand, she shut the car door and marched toward his front steps

But lo and behold, Prince Charming had already bolted out the door and was jogging down the porch steps, running to....

WAIT!

Didn't he realize her dad was in the car, watching? NO! He did that in front of God and everyone. As I was applying the Vulcan Death Grip to the steering wheel, he embraced her and gave her a big hen-peck kiss...on the mouth! Was he nuts?

After disgustingly separating their lips, they both came to the driver's side of my car. Then, after he opened the door like he owned the dang thing, they both—yeah, BOTH—got in the backseat...TOGETHER!

He had kissed my little girl, hugged her, held her hand, and was now sitting in the backseat with her. O yeah, with his arm around her. Was there no end to the madness?

"Dad, this is Jeff," Elle politely introduced him. WOW! *Where did my little girl go?* I wondered. She was kissing boys and being polite. It sure looked like her, but it couldn't have been—could it?

"How are you doing, sir?" Jeff asked as he pulled his arm from behind Elle's shoulders to shake my hand.

Listen, Punk! If I ever see you kiss her again, there will be consequences that you won't like! I don't know if she told you, but I was just paroled from prison, and to tell you the truth, I have no problem going back!

Even though that was a complete lie, that is word-for-word exactly what I would have said had I not made eye contact with my daughter as he extended his hand.

Since I did see her, what I was thinking didn't come out of my mouth quite that way. Unfortunately, it was totally different.

"Hi, Jeff," I said with a smile as I saw Elle in my peripheral vision giving me the same demonic look Sissy Spacek gave in her award-winning performance as *Carrie.*

As if I were driving through a mine field while avoiding flying bullets and exploding grenades, I continued on despite those evil looks. "It is really a pleasure to meet you, young man."

My words came across as sincere and excited. Needless to say, they were far from genuine. While I was greeting him with kindness, I was trying to figure out how I could get a good mug shot of the boy, in my head. After all, the sides of milk cartons and posters would need a good picture if he, for some mysterious reason, came up missing.

With that, we were off to the game. As bad as things seemed, it didn't take long for it to get worse. After I backed out of the driveway, I noticed something disturbing in the rearview mirror. The two of them had started to kiss as I put the car into Drive. As a father, I have never felt so uncomfortable and hurt.

Call it déjà-vu, but I was now living the exact horrifying vision I had seen when Elle was just three days old and pee'd on my leg. They were in the backseat in an all-out mouth open lip-lock—disgusting!

Of course, I did what all calm, cool, and rational dads would do in that particular situation. I sped up a bit, then slammed on my brake.

"OOOHHHHHHHHH!!! Sorry, about that," I said, trying to hide my laughter. "You sure do have a lot of squirrels running around here, don't you, Jeff?"

"Uh—no, not really, sir," he replied. "I guess they can just run around everywhere, though."

For the rest of the five-minute drive to the basketball game, I managed to stay in constant conversation with the young lad. Every thirty seconds or so, I would catch my daughter's *Carrie* eyes telling me to "Shut up!" But for a change, that was fine with me. I had Jeff right where I wanted him.

It pains me to say that Elle and her "older man" did not work out. (Let's be serious! I was ecstatic to see them break up.) For some odd reason, she never again asked me to take her and a boyfriend anywhere. Perhaps it's because her boyfriends just liked talking to me so much that it made her feel left out.

"The most called-upon prerequisite of a friend is an accessible ear."

—Maya Angelou

A Shoestring?

"Hang on," I yelled to Elle as she hurried me so we could go eat breakfast. "I just want to throw these clothes in the dryer."

I hurried to the laundry room and began pulling out clothes. As I tossed them from the dryer into a clothes basket, my daughter was being a typical fourteen-year old, rushing me as impatiently as she could. I was hungry, too, but like any other parent, did I expect an early teen to do anything to help me get this done so we could go? No. She simply stood by the door trying to rush me.

After only a couple of minutes, I had the last bit of clothes from out of the dryer and they were in the basket. As I started to shut the dryer door, I decided to do something I wish I never would have done. I double-checked the dryer to make sure I didn't miss anything.

Sure enough, there was something—a *shoestring*. Why did she wash a shoestring? I rolled my eyes in *typical* disbelief. I reached my hand in to pull it out, hoping it hadn't somehow wound itself inside the machine and broken something. Thankfully, as I grabbed onto the black string, it wasn't wound into a mess and pulled right out. Relieved and feeling my anger exhale, I lifted the....

At that point, I stopped exhaling and even stopped breathing. What I grasped in my right hand was what I had thought was a *string*. Now, I quickly realized it was no string at all. As I brought what I thought belonged in my daughter's shoe to eye level, I felt it was nearly the worst Dad Moment in my parenting life. I could have screamed when I realized this "string" in no way resembled what I had originally thought. That tiny piece of string made me feel as nauseated as when I had discovered what *With Wings* meant. That shoestring was...one of my fourteen-year-old daughter's thongs.

As I had learned in my Padman adventure, there are certain things we men never want to run across in life. This one ranked right up there with catching your parents having sex. Likewise, it was just as despicable. Indeed, some things men should not hear and definitely not see. And, since fatherhood can easily be compared to climbing a ladder, this discovery was the next rung I was being forced to reach. Should I keep climbing or just call an end to all of this madness and ignore it?

Unsure whether I would pull myself up the ladder or lay low and let her mom handle it, another transformation occurred in me when I found...her *shoestring*. Every sexual-thought-inducing vision I had ever smiled at when I had thought of a thong flashed before my eyes; now, those sexual thoughts had turned into deplorable Dad visions.

As I stood over the washer with her *shoestring* on the floor, my body temperature must have risen eighteen degrees; I was furious. Disgusted and angry, I had immediately flung the things out of my hand as if a bee had landed on me.

How could her mom let her have such a thing? Did her mom even know? This absolutely demanded a phone call.

At one time, I had thought a thong was a prestigious sight to behold; it was extremely arousing, almost naughty. As a matter of fact, a lot of men prefer to see their ladies in these scanty undergarments commonly referred to as thongs. There is something ultra sexy about seeing, well, not seeing, anything on one's lady's behind. From the rear, there is a small waistband—nothing else. The frontal view is nearly as sexy. A small, sleek, and did I mention extremely sexy, piece of cloth covers her female region. This piece of cloth is barely enough to canvas the pubic area. Whether intended by the more feminine gender or not, this type of "clothing" is very alluring, almost magnetic to guys. I had always had a genuine appreciation and respect for thong developers—until that precise moment.

Then, all of the sex-intended thoughts changed for me because I saw my daughter's thong; it was flat-out gross. Instantly, these panties became something utterly bizarre. As a dad, I had already made the ultimate transformation and evolved into Padman. But even Padman was not ready for *this*. Thongs, which should be illegal for girls under the age of twenty, were suddenly added to my despicable list. There are restrictions on driving, cigarettes, and liquor, so why not put a "Must Be 20" sign on thongs? It makes sense to us dads, right?

My little girl's lingerie (the phrase makes me shiver as much as the words *Heavy Flow* and *With Wings*) had to be brought to my attention just before Saturday morning breakfast, our weekly ritual. How would I find a way to shut out the thoughts and questions about her panties, pretending this discovery had never happened? As a dad, how was I supposed to do that with my daughter?

In the car, I could feel the tension rising. Don't take that wrong; I was the only one feeling tense, but still....

Elle turned my radio off of sports talk and forced me to listen to some hip-hop group, *Black-Eyed Fruit Salad*, or something like that; I just know it wasn't my music. Fortunately, at that moment, I couldn't even hear the noise. Bewildered during the drive, I just wondered, did a thong mean that my daughter was having sexual thoughts at her young age? I was scared.

When we walked into the restaurant, I was amazed that I had not yet yelled at her for having such a sex thing. *She was only fourteen.* To think she had kept this secret from me while accidentally leaving those things in the wash. As she excused herself to the restroom, I pulled out my cell phone to find out whether her mother knew about this, and if she did, I was sure going to give her a piece of my mind.

"Carrie!" I began as she answered. "Did you know that *your* daughter is wearing thongs? I was washing clothes today and came across one. That's so not...."

Her laughter cut me off. Puzzled, I stopped and asked her what was so funny?

"Girls think it's cool to try and wear them at her age," broke through her laughter. "She's not doing anything wrong. I bought them for her."

"ARE YOU SERIOUS?" I fumed before launching into an interrogating tone that I thought would have intimidated Bin Laden. "Why? Do you know what this can lead to? For the love of God, she's only a child!"

"She's fine, *Dad*," Carrie mocked me, still laughing. "I have to go; we're going to the cabin."

After I hung up the phone, I tried being rational. I tried to think, "Okay, maybe her mom is right. Perhaps I am overanalyzing things. Perhaps this is no big deal. Perhaps...."

"May I take your order?" the waitress interrupted my thoughts.

"I want pancakes," Elle shouted as she made her way back to the table, acting as if nothing had changed. But in my eyes, everything had changed. She was wearing those things and it had to mean something about sex.

"I just want orange juice and toast," I ordered after Elle was finished.

"What's wrong with you, Dad?" my daughter asked as the waitress left to place our order. "Aren't you hungry?"

So, I did what any dad does during trying feminine times with his daughter. I lied, avoided the issue, and just prayed that her mom would take care of it. After all, since I only saw her a couple of days a week, I didn't want to upset her and lose that.

Somehow, I managed to get through breakfast unscathed. On the ride home, though, I tried subtly to release my questions.

"So, Elle," I began with my left hand relaxing on the steering wheel and my right elbow on the arm rest. "Anything new?"

Obviously, that wasn't too slick. As if a red flag popped up over my head, Elle turned to me and demanded to know, "WHY?"

"Just curious how you're doing in school or whatever," I said, calmly.

"Oh, things are fine. Bobby won't leave me alone, but other than that things are great."

"Who's Bobby?" I quickly asked in red-alert fashion.

"He's just this kid at school who thinks I'm his girlfriend, and I've told him over and over there is no way!"

Does he know you wear a thong? Is that why he's interested? I couldn't help wondering.

But the sound of her warding off boys was music to my ears. Seeing how she had told me that, I felt it was safe to continue my line of questioning.

"I found something in the dryer today, Elle," I mentioned before pouring on the Officer Friday grillwork. "Care to explain?"

She looked at me the way a dog in the yard looks at a closed fence.

"Your mom tells me that it's...."

"Are you talking about my thongs?" she casually interrupted me with a laugh. "Mom got those for me. You don't like them?"

Don't like them?

Was she serious?

"Elle, is there a reason you feel the need to wear them?" I asked in complete seriousness.

"Dad? Why are we having this conversation?" she pleaded. "I just like 'em."

"But, honey, it's like dental floss up your butt," I pointed out in my *dad-like* wisdom. "You don't just walk around picking all day?"

"No, Dad!" she, like her mom, laughed at me. "It's nothing like that. Yeah, it's up there, but it just stays."

Right then I stopped. I was not about to have more of a conversation about underwear or panties with my fourteen-year-old daughter. Going by her mom's reaction, thongs were just that, panties. Thongs, briefs, or boxers, they were all the same.

However, in a dad's eyes, they weren't even in the same ballpark.

"All right, Elle," I shifted gears. "As long as your mom says they're okay and not sexual things, I'll be okay with it. But, are you sure there's not more I should know?"

"DADDDD!!!" she shouted. "It's just underwear. You wear boxers, but I don't ask you why, do I?"

She had a point. Her mom had seemed to think the thong was okay, even though I thought it was completely not okay at her age. So, I did the next best thing to making my own decision; I used a lifeline and phoned a friend for help when we pulled back into the driveway.

Following that ten-minute conversation, which I went behind the house and hid to have, I was convinced that it had nothing to do with sexuality. It simply had to do with being cool and comfortable.

I learned a valuable lesson from that *shoestring* incident. As a single father, I could have done what I wanted and thrown a fit, forbidding her ever to wear those things again. I could have made a huge deal out of the situation, and once again, demanded her to follow my orders. But, would she have listened, or would that have pushed her further into rebelling?

As my friend, Rose, so matter-of-factly pointed out on the phone, I was wrong even to make an issue out of it. If I continued, would I be prepared to check her panties every time she showered or changed clothes? Every morning before school? Was I going to hound her every day? Or, was I going to trust that her mom, step dad, and I had instilled good values in her, and she didn't need to be babysat 24/7 like an infant.

That was a valuable lesson I struggled to learn as a father, not to be so overbearing. As Elle would gladly tell anyone, there comes a time when Dad has to let his daughter grow up. The thong incident is just a basic example, but in several other instances throughout her growing up, I had to bite my tongue and not be so overbearing. I'd save flipping out for the bigger issues I feared.

Like...birth control—oh God, did I just think that?

Little Brooke: A TBI Story ALL Parents Need to Read

Some headlines and book titles grab your attention. Others make you shy away from that particular blog, article, or book. The ones that pique your interest enough for you to read them can change your life forever. Along with the first story in this book, this one is aimed at being the latter type. Learning about Traumatic Brain Injuries (TBI) can, and does, have *that* big of an influence on one's thinking.

Have I convinced you yet about the life-changing results from learning about Traumatic Brain Injuries? If not, read about little Brooke....

Even though this book has mostly been an attempt at humor, Traumatic Brain Injuries are anything but a laughing matter. For that reason, this story may be the one many readers will skip; people hate reading about horrible accidents happening to children. Most parents, flat out, do not even want to hear about such accidents because they would, unavoidably, be forced to think about their own children or family members in the same predicament. However, for those of you who do read these final words, hopefully, it will change your outlook before a TBI affects you, your family, or someone you know.

Before delving into this sensitive subject, let's weed out just who is in dire need of seeing what a brain injury is capable of doing. The rest of you can put your worries away and stick with the funny stuff; traumatic brain injuries definitely will never affect you, anyhow. After all, this crippler/killer only— and I do say, only—affects parents, husbands, wives, sisters, brothers, sons, daughters, friends, cousins, servicemen and servicewomen, family members, bosses, co-workers, business owners, alumni, the homeless, nieces, nephews, aunts, uncles, grandmothers, grandfathers, grandchildren, greats of any form, and all people with a pulse. So, unless you happen to fall into one of the aforementioned categories, this book is meaningless to you.

In other words, I guess it is safe to say that not one living human being is immune from a fall, crash, collision, whiplash, or other accident. When these incidents do happen, the sensitivity of the body's control center is revealed.

A very delicate piece of equipment, the brain is encased inside of the skull's rough interior. When the soft brain is forced against this hard and bumpy surface, there will, undoubtedly, be some type of damage. Depending on how hard the brain is slammed against the crater-like skull, the amount of damage will vary. After all, the brain tells us how to think, feel, say, and do. The slightest damage can, subsequently, result in memory loss, speech impairment, and the inability to walk, see, talk, and even, feel.

By finding this book and making the choice to read these stories, your brain was required to make decisions. What if your brain were damaged, rendering you unable to make such small decisions? Then you, yes you, would know what it is like to be severely brain injured. You might not be able to read. You might not be able to comprehend that you like laughter. You might not be able to differentiate between genres. And, you very well might not even be able to hold a book steady in your hands.

Can you imagine it, *yet*?

If you now see how a Traumatic Brain Injury could potentially affect you or someone you love one day, read on. If not, just keep "ignoring" the content.

Either way you choose to look at it, mark my words, if something like TBI ever really happens to a family member of yours, which is a very real possibility, you will not be able to "ignore" it. Odds are, you will learn everything about the brain, how it functions, and how it reacts, just as Brooke's mother, Dianna Stroud, has done since her daughter suffered a life-crippling injury as a wee little girl. Trying to hold back her tears, she recalled for me the 1998 incident involving her three-year old daughter.

"I heard brakes squealing; I heard screaming; I heard everything. As I came around the side of the house, I saw her lying in the middle of the road. I remember running to her. I put my hands on either side of her head and started screaming her name. I did everything I could without moving her to get her to respond. But she wouldn't respond at all."

Brooke's failure to respond turned out to be something that every roadside onlooker feared that day. After Brooke was rushed to the hospital, doctors gave Dianna the worst news she had ever heard.

"Mrs. Stroud," a trauma surgeon began, "your daughter has a 2 percent chance to survive. We don't expect she's going to make it off of the operating table. Would you like to kiss your daughter goodbye?"

Parents: take a second; re-read that last sentence. Then, put yourself in that place.
Can you "ignore" it, now?

Today, thirteen years and nineteen surgeries later, Brooke has beaten the odds and is still with us. Surprisingly, the sixteen-year old is getting by without a portion of her brain. The right frontal lobe had to be completely removed because it was so damaged.

"If a CT Scan were performed, there would be nothing but a big black spot where that part of Brooke's brain was," Dianna pointed out. "When her head was struck by the driver's side mirror, shards of her skull peppered that section of her brain and killed it. The surgeons had to take all of the damaged area out."

Most people think of a car's bumper hitting a person when they think of a car striking someone on foot. Had Brooke been a hair shorter, though, she would have probably been completely fine. The driver's-side mirror, the only part of the car to hit Brooke, would have probably missed her completely. However, the oncoming car, which—brace yourself!—"swerved to miss a squirrel in the road," struck Brooke and its side mirror smashed in the defenseless little girl's head.

Automobile accidents, biking accidents, sports injuries, trip-and-fall accidents, playground incidents, or backyard playtime injuries are all distinct possibilities for head injuries that can cause a brain injury. The chance of suffering such a closed or open head injury is greater than one would like to think. From a mild concussion to death, brain injuries take many shapes and forms. It is up to the parents to understand such injuries should such an incident ever happen to their own child. Dianna, who has basically devoted the last thirteen years to taking care of Brooke, offered a few heart-felt suggestions.

"Never give up hope. No matter how bleak it seems, don't give up," she sincerely began. "Keep talking to them. Play them music you know they listen to, and watch the TV shows they like. Read them books they like. But...just...don't...stop; you never know. They told me, basically, my child was gone. You have to reach down deep inside, and it's going to be the most horrific thing you have to do. It's not your decision, though."

Odds are, Brooke will never walk distances by herself, she will never drive a car, and she will never read a book. Basically, she is looking at a life of dependency. However, based on the happenings of August 17, 1998, following forty days of life support, two and a half months in a coma, long-term twenty-four-hour nurses-aid surveillance, and a 109-day hospital stay, Brooke is a miracle. She can love, she can show emotion, and even though she cannot really communicate through speech, she has the temperament of a typical teenager—just ask Mom.

"I don't cut her any slack," Dianna said with a proud smile. "She's in that wheelchair, but (like all teenagers) she knows how to instigate a fight with her sisters (Brittney and Briana)."

Understand that brain injuries are real and devastating, most often irreconcilable. In everyday life, they are always lurking around the corner. After hearing the story of this beautiful little girl, can you "ignore" it? Can you afford to ignore it?

P.S. Brooke, your mom told me she would read this to you. I also know that she read the entire *Twilight* series to you in two weeks, so I'm pretty sure that you've heard this story by now. I just hope you can somehow understand what she has told you about how you and I share a rare bond, a connection that most people wouldn't *want* to share. I want you always to know that you have a lifelong friend in me. I'm seeing quite a few Hot Fudge Sundae trips in our future.

Story Spoken for All TBI Survivors, Loud and Clear

July 31, 1992 was like any other day for Chris Frasier...
until she answered the phone.

"They [St. Mary's Hospital in Saginaw, Michigan] called
and asked if I had a daughter, Sandra Frasier," the mother of
two remembers. "Then, they said there had been a car
accident. I just handed the phone to Lawrence [husband and
father]; I lost it."

Apparently, Sandra, a twenty-year-old auditor at the time,
was returning to the office from the day's final stop. In
unfamiliar territory, she was trying to scan a map and drive at
the same time. Unfortunately, she didn't see a stop sign and
sped through it as an SUV blasted the side of her Toyota
Camry. She suffered six broken ribs, a broken collarbone, and
a life-threatening traumatic brain injury. Surprisingly to most,
the future mother of Sam, "Don't call me 'Sammy," did not
even have one scratch on her face.

"They had her head bandaged where you could only see the
front of her face, and it was undamaged," Chris explained.
"But from the bandages back, it was as black as you can
imagine. They told us that it was a closed head injury (no
penetrating wound to the head) and there wasn't a direct hit; it
just shook her brain."

Perhaps the most important aspect of Sandra's traumatic
event is something that most people are unaware of, but they

need to learn! Make no mistake—one of the most life- and functional-saving factors that every person *needs* to understand about Traumatic Brain Injury (TBI) is that the faster medical attention is received, the better are the chances for survival. Brain injuries are nothing to gamble with. If attention is not provided immediately, long-term problems, disabilities, and possibly even death may result. In this case, the speedy work of a caring onlooker, police, and medical workers may have saved a life.

Fortunately, one person was standing on his porch at the time of impact. Immediately, he phoned 911. Again, fortunately, a police officer was only a mile away. Just "thirteen" minutes after the crash, Sandra was in a hospital bed and receiving medical attention. As much as anything, it was probably that quick response that saved her life.

Upon arrival at St. Mary's, the Frasiers immediately began facing the dreaded uphill climb. Despite the hospital medical personnel's explanations of how well-known and prestigious the main doctor was, maternal instincts took over immediately as Chris exploded at the other workers after hearing the doctor say, "She'll never leave that bed."

"I DO NOT want that man back in there! If he's that negative, I DON'T want him in her room."

Thus began the grueling journey of another TBI victim, hoping to return to herself.

Parents, other family members, friends, and concerned hospital workers went six nervous weeks waiting, hoping, and praying for a miracle as Sandra remained comatose for that time. Then, after she did finally "wake up," she spent a couple of more weeks with her eyes open and no movement. Following six weeks in Saginaw, Sandra was transferred to Ann Arbor, Michigan, in an ambulance, spending nearly six months in St. Joseph's Hospital. Then, after finally being allowed to return home, she spent over a year in outpatient therapy.

"I just wanted to get back to work so bad," Sandra noted, remembering the events from nineteen years earlier. "I had problems, but I knew I could do this."

As a lifelong volleyball player (her true passion), worker of two jobs, college student, and coach of her favorite sport, there is no doubt that Sandra was a "go-er," as her parents put it. In fact, Mr. and Mrs. Frasier heard their first good news from a nurse because of their daughter's activity-filled past. When the couple was asked how active of a person Sandra was before the accident, they had no problem rattling off a full plate for the 1989 Bendle High School graduate. Upon hearing how involved and busy she was, the nurse proclaimed, "She'll recover rather quickly."

However, as speedy as the initial treatment was and as positive as the nurse seemed, there is nothing—and I do mean n-o-t-h-i-n-g—"fast" about the healing process of a TBI victim. In fact, the harsh reality is that many aspects of an injured brain may never completely heal. For instance, nearly two decades later, Sandra, by her own admission, has a horrible short-term memory, a spotty long-term memory, poor balance, walking problems, poor coordination, affected speech, weak concentration abilities, and attention problems.

For years, her disability worker was a true godsend in Sandra's eyes. This lady helped Sandra fight to regain her life as she struggled to regain some form of independence. Then, that worker accepted a promotion in 2006, so Sandra was assigned to a different worker. Unfortunately, the relationship with the new worker didn't start off so well. In fact, this disability worker proved to be no different than a large portion of the rest of society in showing her ignorance about brain injuries. She exhibited nothing short of true heartless and unsympathetic ignorance. Though the worker will remain nameless because I, personally, don't believe in crucifying people in public—even though her comments deserve it—her words will make the skin crawl on any TBI survivor and his/her family.

Don't believe me?

Ask a severe TBI survivor or that person's family members how they take the words that Sandra was told by her "professional" case worker in 2006. As Sandra was simply trying to find a job she could perform fourteen years after her 1992 accident, she was greeted with colder-than-imaginable words:

"Sandra, your accident was in '92, right? You should be better by now."

Earlier, I noted that n-o-t-h-i-n-g about a TBI is a quick fix. In fact, when the body's entire control center is disrupted, there will be consequences. Making the injury even more mysterious to outsiders is the fact that many of the lingering problems are not visible. Subsequently, a traumatic brain injury is often called the invisible injury.

For instance, a TBI survivor may have trouble walking, talking, memorizing, concentrating, and/or performing numerous other "normal" daily functions. However, once the brain has been damaged, these "simple" functions have to be reprogrammed into the brain. Unfortunately, many instances exist where many of these "normal" activities never come back: e.g., all of the aforementioned functions.

"After I came out of the coma, I just wanted to go back to work," Sandra reminisced. "I knew I didn't belong there."

When asked how much they felt their daughter had transformed back to her *old self*, Chris and Lawrence quickly differed.

"I'd say she's 60-65 percent of what she used to be," Chris optimistically began before being interrupted by Lawrence. "Start with the report at St. Mary's saying she'll never come out of the coma, to six-and-a half months later talking and actually walking with a little help; she does most of her own housekeeping, and she's a wonderful mother—Samantha is her number one priority...."

"Ya think?" Lawrence interjected with a laugh, extremely giddy about his daughter's tremendous strides. "I'd say more like 40-45 percent. She was such a go-er."

"She is married, a great mother to Samantha, and does most things by herself," Chris quickly retorted. "She even ran a daycare for a while with me where she was in control of six children, five in diapers."

Unfortunately, like any severe TBI survivor, Sandra does have some obvious "problems." For example, her speech isn't what she'd like, but she is completely understandable. She has balance problems and has to wear ankle braces every day but, outside of the minor inconvenience of putting on the braces each day—which nobody else would ever even notice—she has walked completely unassisted for years. Then, Lawrence illustrated how her memory is pretty bad. As just one story, he laughingly pointed out that she has resorted to using creative tricks. For instance, she called his house recently, asking for her mom. When Lawrence told Sandra she wasn't home, the forty-year old said, "Okay, just tell her to remember 'garage' and call me when she gets home."

With a strong family and support group around her for every step of her journey, including her parents and her brother Mike, Sandra continues to impress everyone.

"When she got out of the hospital, the *Flint Journal* [local newspaper] was there to take pictures and some people from the high school had put 'Welcome Home' banners up in the yard for Sandra," Chris reflected with a smile. "The school and the community were great. We've received a lot of support and prayers. I still meet people whom I don't know at church who'll say, 'Hey, didn't I pray for your daughter years ago?'"

Fortunately, even if Sandra is "only" 40 percent of what she was, she's 40 percent more than she *could* have been. Obviously, she has overcome numerous obstacles and has displayed a true warrior mentality in every sense of the word. Anyone who knows Sandra is proud of what she has accomplished as she continues to amaze everyone.

Following are just a few of the stories Sandra and her parents shared with laughter:

On Occupational Therapy (O.T.)—re-learning the decision-making process:

Sandra: "I hated O.T. I would ask her [the therapist] something and she would always say, 'What do you think? I want you to make that decision.' I **hated** that. If I knew, I wouldn't have asked you."

On going for wheelchair rides, which Sandra loved while in St. Joseph's:

Lawrence: "She couldn't hold up her head all the time. It would fall down to the side. As they were building strength up, she loved going for wheelchair rides. So, they'd put towels above her shoulder to keep her head up when I'd push her around for a ride. Then, as she got stronger, they took the towels away. Then, if her head would start falling, I'd tell her, 'You get that head up or I'm taking you back in!'"

On trying to get out of physical therapy:

Lawrence: "We were still down in St. Joe's. She'd been down there a little while, but she was still in a wheelchair. She DIDN'T like going to physical therapy because they used to stretch and pull her arms and legs."

Sandra: "I hated that so bad." (laugh)

Lawrence: (laughing) "She said, 'Dad, Dad, tell 'em my arm hurts today.' I said, 'Okay, I'll tell 'em.'" Then she said, 'Tell 'em it REALLY hurts.' So, (laughing) I said, 'Okay, I'll tell 'em. Then she said, (whisper) 'Dad, Dad, tell 'em it's broke.' (All four of us are rolling.) I tell her, 'I'm not going to tell them that, Sandra.' It was just so painful to watch her have to do stuff she had to do to get better."

On memory problems and disciplining Sam:

Chris: "One time, I told Samantha, 'You better watch out and not talk back. You're going to get into more trouble and you're already grounded tomorrow.' But she came back with, 'Nah! Mom will forget.'" (all laugh)

Sandy: "So I wrote on the calendar, 'Grounded Tomorrow.'" (all laugh)

Me: "It's so nice to see you and your parents laughing so much at these typical problems. You have to be able to laugh about it. There's nothing we can do so we have to laugh."

Lawrence: "Oh, we do all the time. You have to."

Me: "If I ran around frustrated and ticked off at all of my memory problems and deficits I have, I'd live a miserable life. We HAVE to laugh at it to cope."

On getting better and on with life:

Sandra: "I just wanted to get better so I could go home and get back to work; I knew I could do it. My work was waiting for me."

On saying one thing about TBI victims:

Sandra: "We're different, but we're not retarded. It might just take a little longer to sink in. If someone tells a joke, it might take me a little longer to get it."

Lawrence: "Sandra's always saying, 'I just wish they'd treat me like everyone else.'"

Dear Reader -- a letter from Mark Elswick

Dear Reader,

Don't you hate to hear a "but" follow a compliment? For example, "She's beautiful and all, BUT... or he is so smart and has a tremendous future, BUT...." Well, numerous readers have responded to the e-book version of *Padman* by stating, "That's a really funny book, BUT it's promoting traumatic brain injury?"

Actually, the point is to promote traumatic brain injury *recovery*, with humor and sometimes yes even bad taste. Why does this matter? Simply because what one person makes possible becomes possible for ALL people. For example, before the record for the four-minute mile was broken, doctors said it was physiologically impossible. Then on May 6, 1954, Roger Bannister proved them wrong. Since then, more than 855 have broken that record. Coincidence? Maybe not!

Of course, I'm not stating that 100 percent recovery is possible for all TBI survivors or even any, but the one thing I can guarantee is this: recovery ONLY comes to those who work for it. If this book gives hope to even one survivor or his or her family to "go for the gold," then I have achieved my desire.

What those naysayers fail to realize is the power of laughter. For instance, if someone is at a funeral, gets hurt, or hears horrible news, what happens? Yep! Sadness and tears. Conversely, if that person sees his favorite movie, eats his favorite dinner, or receives a promotion at work, what happens? Yep! Smiles and laughter.

As crazy as it may seem to create a mostly humorous book promoting TBI awareness, that is indeed exactly what I intended. Non-believers of this book's purpose are not realizing that laughter heals our hearts and minds, makes our healing process smoother, and helps us transition into a comfortable state.

Although the actual injury and its lingering effects are far from funny, it is what it is; we've been dealt a raw deal in life and have no choice but to accept our circumstances. When life throws lemons at you, make lemonade. For instance, if I didn't laugh at myself because of my memory, balance, coordination, speech, and other problems, and instead, I held onto my hostility, anger, and vengeance, I would probably be one of the most miserable people on the face of the earth.

Believe me, and remember, I'm not an "outsider" preaching to you; I'm one of you—it's not an easy thing to do to let go of your frustration, pain, and embarrassment for not being 100 percent who you were before your accident. But, when you finally accept your lot in life, you will laugh more and be on your way to who you actually are, while probably, maybe surprisingly, you will also be a better human being.

There are so many things that we TBI survivors can't do today that we often lose sight of just what we *can* do. Of course, it's harder than anyone can ever imagine finally to *accept* what we can't do. But when you can accept the fact that you're not the same as you were, be open about it, and understand that it's okay to have some problems out of your control, then you can finally be thankful for what you have— not what you lost!

If I could offer any advice to my TBI brothers and sisters, I would simply say this: The past is the past; leave it there! The future is where you're headed. Don't dwell on what you can't do; dwell on what you *can* and *will* do.

> With Love,
> Mark Elswick
> PROUD Nineteen-Year TBI Survivor

About the Author

"Mr. and Mrs. Elswick, if he has any brothers or sisters, get them up here. He won't make it through the day."

That was the news that greeted Mark E. Elswick's parents upon arrival at the hospital following their only son's automobile accident in September 9, 1992. After the initial prognosis was reported in a small, quiet, closet-like waiting room, the comatose author-to-be's  parents were told that *if* he ever regained consciousness from what turned out to be a month-long coma, Mark would be a vegetable.

Surprisingly, he has defied that immediate "death sentence" and vegetative prediction. Today, Elswick has not only survived, but he has exceeded any possible expectations for a severely brain-injured patient. In addition to retraining his brain to think, eat, walk, and talk, he returned to college, where he had completed his sophomore year before the accident. Against all odds, he went on to earn his B.A. and M.A. from the University of Michigan—Flint and Central Michigan University, respectively.

As an author, Elswick is giving back to the injury which nearly killed him, one book at a time. A percentage of the proceeds from every sale of this book will be donated to Traumatic Brain Injury (TBI) research.

Coming March, 2012:
Traumatic Brain Injuries: Milestones in Recovery

Give to the Brain Injury Association of America Now!

Most people don't know how important they are to the Brain Injury Association of America and the 2 million children and adults who acquire a brain injury in the U.S. each year.

Imagine what life would be like if no one answered the call when an individual with a brain injury or a family member needs help and support.

Imagine there being no information or resources for individuals who have sustained brain injuries.

Imagine what life would be like if publicly-funded research or services for civilians and service members with brain injuries suddenly evaporated.

Imagine there being no education for caregivers, clinicians, business leaders, or attorneys.

Imagine what life would be like if a unified, nationwide voice for brain injury did not exist.

Your generous support means no one has to imagine life under these circumstances. You make it possible for the Brain Injury Association of America to bring help, hope, and healing to millions of people whose lives are forever changed by brain injury.

Donate Online

The Brain Injury Association of America subscribes to Give Direct to make online donations fast, easy, and secure. When you make a donation using VISA or MasterCard, Give Direct does not charge fees to you or BIAA so every dollar you give goes right where you intended. A low fee of 2.85% is deducted from donations made using American Express. With Give Direct, you can give with confidence. Simply visit www.biausa.org and click on the green button to "Donate & Support."

Donate by Phone or Mail

You can make a tax-deductible contribution by phone or mail. Please fill out the Donation Form found on www.biausa.org and mail the form along with your check to:

> Brain Injury Association of America
> 1608 Spring Hill Road, Suite 110
> Vienna, VA 22182

To make a donation over the telephone, please call the Brain Injury Association of America at 703-761-0750 and have your credit card handy.

The Reflections of America Series

Soul Clothes by Regina D. Jemison

Tales of Addiction and Inspiration for Recovery:
Twenty True Stories from the Soul
by Barbara Sinor, PhD

Saffron Dreams by Shaila Abdullah

Confessions of a Trauma Junkie: My Life as a Nurse
Paramedic by Sherry Jones Mayo

My Dirty Little Secrets—Steroids, Alcohol, and God
by Tony Mandarich

The Stories of Devil-Girl by Anya Achtenberg

How to Write a Suicide Note:
serial essays that saved a woman's life
by Sherry Quan Lee

Chinese Blackbird by Sherry Quan Lee

Padman:
A Dad's Guide to Buying...Those and Other Tales
by Mark Elswick

For more information and additional titles, visit:
www.ModernHistoryPress.com

Quick Order Form

$14.95 -- *Padman: A Dad's Guide to Buying . . . Those and other tales*

* let me know by phone, email, or on www.markelswick.com where you heard about *Padman* and receive a $3.00 discount *

Phone Orders: (810) 293-4809; have your credit card ready.

Email Orders: mark@markelswick.com

Postal Orders: send check or money-order to **Mark Elswick:** PO Box 955, Davison, MI 48423-0955

Name: _____

Address: _____

_____

City, State, Zip: _____

Telephone: _____

Email address:_____

Sales tax: Please add 6% for books shipped to Michigan addresses

Shipping fee:
U.S.: $3.00 for first book and $2.00 for each additional book
International: $8.00 for first book and $5.00 for each additional book